ACCOUNTING & AUDITING RESEARCH

A PRACTICAL 4E GUIDE

THOMAS R. WEIRICH, PHD, CPA
PROFESSOR OF ACCOUNTING, CENTRAL MICHIGAN UNIVERSITY

ALAN REINSTEIN, DBA, CPA
PROFESSOR OF ACCOUNTING, WAYNE STATE UNIVERSITY

SOUTH-WESTERN College Publishing

An International Thomson Publishing Company

Sponsoring Editor: David L. Shaut
Production Editor: Michael J. Busam
Production House: DPS Associates, Inc.
Cover Design: Tin Box Studio/Sandy Weinstein
Marketing Manager: Steven W. Hazelwood

ISBN: 0-538-86133-9

Library of Congress Cataloging-in-Publication Data

Weirich, Thomas R.
    Accounting and auditing research : a practical guide / Thomas R.
    Weirich, Alan Reinstein.
        p.   m.
      ISBN 0-538-86133-9 (soft cover)
      1. Accounting—Research. 2. Auditing—Research. I. Reinstein,
    Alan. II. Title.
    HF5630.W39   1995
    657' .072—dc20   95-38695
                                                                CIP

1 2 3 4 5 5 7 8 9 MA 3 2 1 0 9 8 7 6 5

Printed in the United States of America

I(T)P
International Thomson Publishing
South-Western College Publishing is an ITP Company. The ITP trademark is
used under license.

ABOUT THE AUTHORS

Thomas R. Weirich, PhD, CPA, received his B.S. and MBA degrees from Northern Illinois University, and a Doctorate in Accountancy from the University of Missouri-Columbia. He is currently the Arthur Andersen & Co. Alumni Professor of Accounting at Central Michigan University. Dr. Weirich has served on special assignment as the Academic Fellow to the Office of Chief Accountant at the U.S. Securities and Exchange Commission in Washington, D.C. He has public accounting experience with an international firm as well as with a local firm. He has served on the Editorial Advisory board to the Journal of Accountancy as well as a committee member on the American Accounting Association's Education Committee and the SEC Liaison Committee. He is completing an assignment on the AICPA's SEC Regulation's Committee. Professor Weirich has written numerous articles in professional journals and has served as a business consultant to a manufacturing concern. Dr. Weirich has also served eleven years on the Mt. Pleasant, Michigan, City Commission and as mayor of the city. Professor Weirich has been the recipient of the School of Accounting's Outstanding Teacher Award, the College of Business Dean's Teaching Award and the Michigan Association of Governing Boards' Distinguished Faculty Award. He has served as an expert witness for the SEC and other cases.

Alan Reinstein, DBA, CPA, received his B.A. and M.S. degrees from the State University of New York (New Paltz), an MBA degree from the University of Detroit, and a Doctorate in Accounting from the University of Kentucky. He is a Professor in the Department of Accounting, School of Business at Wayne State University. Professor Reinstein conducts many seminars for the AICPA, MACPA, many other state CPA societies and professional groups. An author of more than 100 articles, Dr. Reinstein serves on the editorial boards of several academic and professional journals and on the boards of the Michigan Associations of CPAs, and the Detroit Chapters of the Institute of Internal Auditors and the National Associations of Accountants. He also has chaired the Professional Examination Committee of the American Accounting Association and served on the Task Force on Professional Examinations and Regulations of the Accounting Education Change Commission. Formerly with an international CPA firm, he now functions as a research and educational consultant for many CPAs and attorneys.

PREFACE

This fourth edition of *Accounting and Auditing Research: A Practical Guide* incorporates two new major features. The first is a new chapter on the importance of critical thinking and effective writing skills in conducting accounting or auditing research. The second new feature is the discussion of utilizing the Internet (the "electronic superhighway") for research purposes. The Electronic Frontiers Foundation has provided permission to include with this text a 200+ page Internet text on disk that explains in detail the use of the Internet.

With continued cooperation from Disclosure Incorporated, this edition of the text includes an updated and expanded student version of software and a database developed by Disclosure. This optional student disk contains a comprehensive, interactive, menu-driven software and database that incorporates financial data for various public companies that file with the SEC. The new companies selected for inclusion in this expanded student version include companies that reported topics normally discussed in an intermediate accounting, advanced accounting, or auditing courses. Topics include such issues as discontinued operations, debt restructuring, derivatives, pensions, foreign currencies, purchase or pooling-of-interest accounting, audit opinions, and many more.

The approach of this edition, continued from earlier editions, is that of a do-it-yourself, understand-it-yourself manual that serves as a primer on research methodology to assist the student or practitioner in conducting research to develop solutions to accounting or auditing questions. This text utilized by a number of universities and staff training courses in public accounting firms and corporations guides the reader, step-by-step, through the research process.

New or updated features of the fourth edition include the following:

- A new chapter on the importance of critical thinking and effective writing skills in the research process.
- A new section that discusses the use of the Internet for accounting and auditing research.
- The inclusion of a comprehensive listing of locations on the Internet for accounting and auditing information.
- An updated and expanded student version of the Disclosure software and database.
- Comprehensive chapter updates.

The text has been restructured to incorporate critical thinking and effective writing skills and the use of the Internet. Chapter 1 presents an introduction to accounting and auditing research and highlights the importance of effective research through a discussion of an SEC's enforcement action against an accountant relating to research. The new Chapter 2 presents a discussion of critical thinking and effective writing skills and their implications in accounting and auditing research. Chapters 3 and 4 present an overview of the environment of accounting and auditing research by highlighting the hierarchy of generally accepted accounting principles (GAAP), the standard setting process, and primary and secondary sources of support. Chapter 5 presents a comprehensive discussion and examples of the many sources of authoritative literature. Chapter 6 is an expanded presentation and discussion of major computerized databases available for utilization in accounting and auditing research. This chapter also includes the discussion on the use of the Internet in conducting research. Chapter 7, with the updated and expanded student disk, presents the Disclosure software and database with instructions for its use. Chapter 8 concludes the text by providing a step-by-step approach to conducting accounting/auditing research by presenting a comprehensive case study.

The authors would like to express our continued appreciation to the many users of the previous editions that have provided helpful suggestions of which many have been incorporated into this fourth edition. We also appreciate the technical support provided by the staff of South-Western College Publishing, especially Mike Busam. Finally, special thanks goes to our family members who provided special encouragement during the writing of this edition: Sharon, Laurie, Lisa, Missy, Michelle, Kirsten, and Mara, Shelly, Frank, and Natie.

Thomas R. Weirich
Central Michigan University

Alan Reinstein
Wayne State University

C O N T E N T S

F I G U R E S

C H A P T E R 1

INTRODUCTION TO ACCOUNTING AND AUDITING RESEARCH

Learning Objectives

After completing this chapter, you should understand:

- The definition of accounting/auditing research.

- The nature of accounting/auditing research.

- The importance of critical-thinking and effective communication skills.

- The U.S. Securities & Exchange Commission's view on the importance of research.

- The importance of the economic consequences of standards setting in the research process.

- The role of research within a public accounting firm or within an accounting department of a business or governmental entity.

- The basic steps of the research process.

1

Varying views and interpretations as to the meaning of the term *research* exist among individuals. To many outside accounting and auditing, *research* conveys the picture of an academic researcher preparing a scholarly paper. To others, the term depicts a scientist, in a white lab coat, experimenting with a new miracle drug. In accounting and auditing, "research" points to what the accounting practitioner does as a normal, everyday part of his/her job. The professional accountant, whether in public accounting, industry, or government, frequently becomes involved with the investigation and analysis of an accounting or auditing issue. Resolving these issues requires a clear definition of the problem, gathering information, reviewing authoritative literature, evaluating alternatives, and drawing conclusions. This research process oftentimes requires an analysis of very complex and detailed accounting and/or auditing issues. Therefore, the researching of such an issue will challenge the *critical-thinking* abilities of the professional. That is, the professional must possess the expertise to understand the problem and related facts and render a professional judgment as to a solution for which, in certain cases, no single definitive answer or solution exists. In such cases, the researcher would apply reasonable and reflective thinking in the development of an answer to the issue or problem at hand.

Critical Thinking and Effective Communication

The researcher needs to know "how to think." That is, one should be able to gather the facts, analyze the situation or issue, synthesize and evaluate alternatives, and then develop an appropriate solution. Such skills are essential for the professional accountant to provide his/her services in today's complex, dynamic, and changing profession. In such an environment, the professional accountant must possess the ability to think critically, which includes the ability to understand a variety of contents and circumstances, and to be able to apply and adapt various accounting, auditing, and business concepts and principles to these circumstances in the development of a solution to an issue. The development and nurturing of these critical-thinking skills will also aid an individual in the process of lifelong learning.

Certain research efforts may culminate in memos to workpapers, letters to clients, journal articles, company or firm monographs, or even textbooks. The dissemination of your research, in whatever form, will require the researcher to possess *effective communication skills*, both orally and in writing. The following statement issued in a white paper by the managing partners of selected international public accounting firms stresses the importance of good communication skills, which the professional accountant/auditor should possess:

> Public accounting requires its practitioners to be able to transfer and receive information with ease. Practitioners must be

able to present and defend their views through formal and informal, written and oral, presentation . . . . Practitioners must be able to listen effectively to gain information and understand opposing points of view. They also will need the ability to locate, obtain and organize information from both human and electronic sources.[1]

Your research output must be coherent and concise, incorporate good use of standard English, and be appropriate to the intended reader. Critical-thinking and effective writing skills are the focus of Chapter 2.

What Is Research?

The term *research* has frequently been misunderstood by those unfamiliar with the research process. Such misconceptions perceive research as a mechanical process conducted in a mystical environment by strange individuals. However, the approach is anything but mystical or mechanical. The process of conducting any type of research, including practical accounting and auditing research, is simply a systematic investigation of an issue or problem utilizing the accountant's professional judgment.

The two generalized research problems presented below can provide an insight into the types of research questions confronting the accountant/ auditor:

1. A client is engaged primarily in commercial and agricultural land sales. The company recently acquired a retail land sales project under an agreement stating that, if the company did not desire to pursue the project further, the property could be returned with no liability to the company.

    After considerable investment of money into the project, the state of the economy concerning retail land sales declines and the company decides to return the land. As a result, the client turns to you, the CPA, and requests the proper accounting treatment of the returned project. In question is whether the abandonment represents a disposal of a segment of the business, an unusual and nonrecurring extraordinary loss, or an ordinary loss.
2. As controller for a construction contracting company, you are faced with the following problem. The company pays for rights allowing the contractor to extract a specified volume of landfill from a project for a specified period of time. How should the payments for such landfill rights be classified in the company's financial statements?[2]

---

1   Kullburg, Duane R., William L. Gladstone, Peter R. Scanlon, J. Michael Cook, Ray J. Groves, Larry D. Horner, Shaun F. O'Malley, and Edward A. Kangas, *Perspectives on Education: Capabilities for Success in the Accounting Profession,* April 1989, p. 6.

2   AICPA *Technical Practice Aids,* Vol. 1, Chicago, Commerce Clearing House, Inc.

Research in general can be classified into two primary categories: (1) *pure research* and (2) *applied research*. *Pure research*, often labeled basic or theoretical research, involves the investigation of questions that appear interesting to the researcher, generally an academician, but may have little or no practical application at the present time. For example, a researcher may be interested in the market's reaction to earnings announcements of certain firms in the oil and gas industry.[3] Such research has little present practical application and can be referred to as *empirical research,* i.e., research based upon experiment or observation. However, pure or basic research should not be discounted as worthless. On the contrary, such research adds to the body of knowledge in a particular field and may ultimately contribute directly or indirectly to practical problem solutions. Empirical research studies, for example, are frequently reviewed and evaluated by standard-setting bodies in drafting authoritative accounting and auditing pronouncements.

Applied research, which is the focus of this text, involves the investigation of an issue of immediate practical importance. For example, assume that a public accounting firm has been asked to evaluate a client's proposed new accounting treatment for environmental costs. The client expects an answer within two days as to the acceptability of the new method and the impact it would have on the financial statements. In such a case, a member of the accounting firm's professional staff would investigate to determine if the authoritative literature addresses the issue. If no authoritative pronouncement can be found, the accountant would develop a theoretical justification for, or against, the new method.

The applied research in the preceding example can be categorized as *a priori* (before the fact): The research is conducted before the client actually enters into the transaction. On the other hand, a client may request advice relating to a transaction that has already been executed. Research relating to a completed transaction or other past event is referred to as *a posteriori* (after the fact) research. Frequently, there are advantages to conducting a priori as opposed to a posteriori research. For example, if research reveals that a proposed transaction will have an unfavorable impact on financial statements, the transaction can be abandoned or possibly restructured to avoid undesirable consequences. These options are not available, however, once a transaction is completed.

There is a need to conduct both pure and applied research. If either type of research is conducted properly, the methodology is the same, only the environment differs. Both types of research require sound research design to resolve the issue under investigation effectively and efficiently. No matter how sophisticated an individual becomes in any aspect of accounting or auditing, there will always be problems associated with research. In such situations, the basic research approach developed by the novice researcher can demonstrate his/her competence as a trained professional.

---

3   Bandyopadhyay, Sati P., "Market Reaction to Earnings Announcements of Successful Efforts and Full Cost Firms in the Oil and Gas Industry," *The Accounting Review,* Vol. 69, No. 4 (October 1994), pp. 657–674.

Research Questions

Individual companies or CPA firms conduct private research to resolve specific accounting or auditing issues relating to the company or the CPA's client. The results of this research often lead to new policies or procedures in the application of existing authoritative literature. In this research process, the practitioner (researcher) must answer the following basic questions:

1. Do I have the knowledge to answer the question without conducting research, or must I consult authoritative references?
2. What is authoritative literature?
3. Does authoritative literature address the issue under review?
4. If authoritative literature does exist, where can I find it and develop a conclusion efficiently and effectively?
5. If there exists more than one alternative or more than one authoritative source, which alternative do I select, or what is the hierarchy of authoritative support?
6. If authoritative literature does not exist, what approach do I follow in arriving at a conclusion?

The purpose of this text is to provide the understanding and the research skills needed to answer these questions. The "what's," "why's," and "how's" of practical accounting and auditing research are discussed with emphasis on the following topics: How do I apply a practical research methodology in a timely manner? What are generally accepted accounting principles and generally accepted auditing standards? What constitutes substantial authoritative support? What are the available sources and the hierarchy of authority of current accounting and auditing literature? What databases are available for computer retrieval as an aid to researching a particular problem? What role can the Internet (the information superhighway) have in the research process? A practical research approach is presented along with discussions of various research tools. This research approach is demonstrated through the use of a number of practical problems presented as case studies. The text also presents the importance of critical-thinking and effective writing skills that the researcher should possess in executing the research process. Specific "tips" on these skills are presented in subsequent chapters.

Nature of Accounting and Auditing Research

This text focuses on accounting and auditing research within the practicing segment of the accounting profession, in contrast to theoretical research often conducted by academicians. Today's practitioner must be able to conduct properly and systematically the research required to arrive at appropriate and timely conclusions regarding the issues at hand. Efficient and effective accounting or auditing research is often necessary in order to determine the proper recording, classification, and disclosure of economic events; to determine compliance with authoritative accounting or auditing pronouncements; or to determine the preferability of alternative accounting procedures.

Additional examples of issues frequently encountered by the practitioner include such questions as: What are the accounting or auditing implications of a new transaction? Does the accounting treatment of the transaction conform with generally accepted accounting principles? What are the financial statement disclosure requirements? What is the auditor's association and responsibility when confronted with supplemental information presented in annual reports but not as part of the basic financial statements? Responding to these often complex questions has become more difficult and time-consuming as the financial accounting and reporting requirements and the auditing standards increase in number and complexity. The research process often is complicated further when the accountant or auditor researches a practical issue for which no authoritative literature exists, or the authoritative literature does not directly address the question.

As a researcher, the practitioner should possess certain desired characteristics or attributes that aid in the research process. These characteristics include inquisitiveness, open-mindedness, patience, thoroughness, and perseverance.[4] The researcher needs to be inquisitive while gathering the information needed to obtain a clearer picture of the research problem. Proper problem definition is the most critical component in research. An improperly stated issue or problem often leads to the wrong conclusion or solution no matter how carefully the research process was executed. Likewise, the researcher should be open-minded, so as not to draw conclusions before the research process is completed. A preconceived solution can result in biased research in which the researcher merely seeks evidence to support a preconceived position rather than searching for the most appropriate solution. The researcher must examine the facts, obtain and review authoritative literature, evaluate alternatives, and then draw conclusions based upon research evidence. The execution of an efficient research project takes patience and thoroughness. This is emphasized in the planning stage of the research process, whereby all relevant factors are identified and all extraneous data or "noise" is controlled. Finally, the researcher must work persistently in order to finish the research on a timely basis. Perhaps the most important characteristic of the research process is its ability to add to the value of the services provided by the accountant or auditor. A good auditor not only renders an opinion on a client's financial statements, but also identifies available reporting alternatives that may benefit the client. The ability of a researcher to provide such information becomes more important as the competition among accounting firms for clients becomes more intense. Researchers who identify reporting alternatives that provide benefits or avoid pitfalls will provide a strong competitive edge to the firm that employs them. Providing these tangible benefits to clients

---

4   Wallace, Wanda, "A Profile of a Researcher," *Auditor's Report*, American Accounting
    Association (Fall 1984), pp. 1–3.

through careful and thorough research is an outstanding method of differentiating a firm's services from those of its competitors.

Economic Consequences of Standards Setting

It has become apparent that various accounting standards can bring about far-reaching economic consequences, as has been demonstrated by the Financial Accounting Standards Board (FASB) in addressing such issues as income taxes, financial instruments, stock options, and post-employment benefits. In evaluating these and other concerns, various difficulties often can arise in the proper accounting for the economic substance of a transaction within the current accounting framework.

In the allocation of resources in today's capital markets, many different types of information are available. Of particular interest to many allocation decisions is the use of financial information reported via an entity's financial statements. Since these financial statements must conform to generally accepted accounting principles, the standard-setting bodies, such as the FASB, will conduct careful and comprehensive research in the development of a proposed standard due to its economic impact on the resource allocation decisions of investors and creditors in today's capital markets. Greater emphasis by standards-setting authorities is being placed upon the cost/benefit issues for the entity and society as a whole when contemplating the issuance of a new accounting standard. For example, the handling of off-balance sheet transactions at times has forced the selection of one business decision over another, which often produces results that may be less oriented to the users of financial statements.

Therefore, the researcher conducting accounting and auditing research needs to be cognizant of the economic and social impact that various accepted accounting alternatives may have on society and in particular on the individual entity. Such economic and social concerns are becoming a greater factor in the evaluation and issuance of new accounting standards, as discussed more thoroughly in Chapter 3.

Role of Research in the Accounting Firm

Although research is often conducted by accountants in education, industry, or government, accounting and auditing research is particularly important in the public accounting firm. Due to the number and diversity of clients served, public accounting firms constantly engage in research on a wide range of accounting and auditing issues.

As a reflection of today's society, significant changes have occurred in the accounting environment. Greater knowledge is required by the practitioner today because of greater complexity in many business transactions and the proliferation of new authoritative pronouncements. As a result, practitioners should possess the ability to conduct efficient accounting and auditing research. An analogy can be drawn between an accountant's responsibility to conduct accounting/auditing research and an attorney's responsibility to conduct legal research. Rule One of the Model Rules of Professional Conduct of the American Bar Association states:

> A lawyer should provide competent representation to a client. Competent representation requires the legal knowledge, skill, thoroughness, and preparation reasonably necessary for the representation.

In a California court decision, this rule was interpreted to mean that each lawyer must be able to completely research the law and is expected to know "those plain and elementary principles of law which are commonly known by well-informed attorneys and to discover the rules which, although not commonly known, may readily be found by standard research techniques."[5]

In this case, the plaintiff recovered a judgment of $100,000 in a malpractice suit that was based upon the malpractice of the defendant lawyer in researching the applicable law.

The U.S. Securities & Exchange Commission (SEC) has also stressed the importance of effective accounting research through an enforcement action brought against an accountant. In *Accounting and Auditing Enforcement Release No. 420* (September, 1992), the SEC instituted a public administrative proceeding against a CPA. The Commission charged that the CPA failed to exercise due care in the conduct of an audit. The enforcement release specifically stated the following:

> In determining whether the (company) valued the lease properly, the (CPA) failed to consult pertinent provisions of GAAP or any other accounting authorities. This failure to conduct any research on the appropriate method of valuation constitutes a failure to act with due professional care. . . .

Thus, it is vital for the accountant/auditor to possess the ability to find and locate applicable authoritative pronouncements and to ascertain their current status. The purpose of this text is to aid the researcher in meeting this objective.

Due to this expanding complex environment and proliferation of pronouncements, certain accounting firms have created a specialization in the research function within the firm. Common approaches used in practice include the following: (1) The staff at the local office conducts day-to-day research with industry-specific questions referred to industry specialists within the firm; (2) selected individuals in the local or regional office are designated as research specialists

---

5   Smith and Lewis, 13 Cal. 3d 349, 530 P.2d 589, 118 Cal Reptr. 621 (1975).

and all research questions within the office or region are brought to their attention for research; and (3) the accounting firm establishes at the executive office
of the firm a centralized research function that handles questions for the firm as a
whole on technical issues. The task of accurate and comprehensive research can
be complex and challenging. However, one can meet the challenge by becoming
familiar with a methodology of conducting selected steps (a research process) in
the attempt to solve an accounting or auditing issue.

A more in-depth look at a typical organizational structure for policy decision
making and research on accounting and auditing matters within a multioffice
firm that maintains a research department is depicted in Figure 1-1

The responsibilities of a firm-wide accounting and auditing policy decision
function include maintaining a high level of professional competence in accounting and auditing matters; developing and rendering high-level policies and procedures on accounting and auditing issues for the firm; disseminating the firm's
policies and procedures to appropriate personnel within the firm on a timely
basis; and supervising the quality control of the firm's practice. Research plays
an important role in this decision-making process.

The Policy Committee and Executive Subcommittee, as shown in Figure 1-1,
generally consist of highly competent partners with many years of practical

FIGURE 1-1   Organizational Framework for Policy Decision Making
and Research Within a Typical Multioffice Accounting
Firm

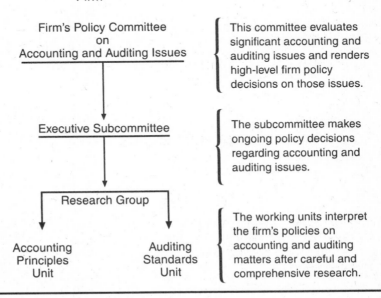

Firm's Policy Committee
on
Accounting and Auditing Issues

This committee evaluates
significant accounting and
auditing issues and renders
high-level firm policy
decisions on those issues.

Executive Subcommittee

The subcommittee makes
ongoing policy decisions
regarding accounting and
auditing issues.

Research Group

The working units interpret
the firm's policies on
accounting and auditing
matters after careful and
comprehensive research.

Accounting
Principles
Unit

Auditing
Standards
Unit

experience. The Policy Committee's primary function is to evaluate significant accounting and auditing issues and establish firm-wide policies on these issues. The Executive Subcommittee function is to handle the daily ongoing policy decisions (lower-level decisions) for the firm as a whole. The responsibility of the accounting and auditing research units is to interpret firm policies in the context of specific client situations. Frequently, technical accounting and auditing issues that arise during the course of a client engagement can be resolved through research conducted by personnel assigned to the engagement. When a matter cannot be resolved satisfactorily at the local-office level, assistance is requested from the firm's research units. These units conduct careful and comprehensive research in arriving at the firm's response to technical inquiries. The firm's response is then disseminated to the various offices of the firm for future reference in handling similar technical issues.

Practical accounting and auditing research is not confined to the public accounting firm. All accountants should possess the ability to conduct efficient research and develop logical and well-supported conclusions on a timely basis. The research process is identical, whether the researcher is engaged in public accounting, management accounting, internal auditing, not-for-profit, or governmental accounting or auditing. Thus the process remains the same; only the environment differs.

Overview of the Research Process

The research process in general is often defined as the scientific method of inquiry, a systematic study of a particular field of knowledge in order to discover scientific facts or principles. The basic purpose of research, therefore, is to obtain knowledge or information that specifically pertains to some issue or problem. An operational definition of research encompasses the following elements:[6]

1. There must be an orderly investigation and analysis of a clearly defined issue or problem.
2. An appropriate scientific approach must be used.
3. Adequate and representative evidence must be gathered and documented.
4. Logical reasoning must be employed in drawing conclusions.
5. The researcher must be able to support the validity or reasonableness of the conclusions.

With this general understanding of the research process, practical accounting and auditing research may be defined as follows:

> *Accounting or auditing research*—A systematic and logical approach employing critical-thinking skills to obtain and document evidence underlying a conclusion relating to an

---

6   Luck, David J., Hugh C. Wales, and Donald A. Taylor, *Marketing Research,* (Englewood Cliffs: Prentice-Hall, Inc., 1961), p. 5.

accounting or auditing issue or problem currently confronting the accountant or auditor.

The basic steps in the research process are illustrated in Figure 1-2 with an
overview presented in the following sections. As indicated in the illustration,
each step of the research process should be documented carefully; the steps in the
research process are closely interrelated. In the actual process of executing each
step, it may also be necessary to refine the work done in previous steps. The
refinement of the research process is discussed more fully in Chapter 8.

FIGURE 1-2   The Research Process

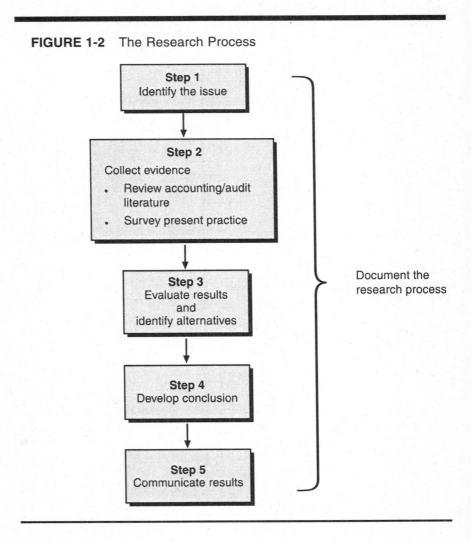

Step 1
Identify the issue

Step 2
Collect evidence
• Review accounting/audit
  literature
• Survey present practice

Step 3
Evaluate results
and
identify alternatives

Step 4
Develop conclusion

Step 5
Communicate results

Document the
research process

Identify the Issue.   The researcher's first task is to gather the facts surrounding the particular problem. However, problem-solving research cannot begin until the researcher has clearly and concisely defined the problem.   One needs to know the "why" and "what" about the issue in order to begin the research process.   Unless you know why the issue is brought to your attention, you might have difficulty knowing what to research. The novice researcher will find it difficult to distinguish between relevant and irrelevant information. It is advisable to err on the side of gathering too many facts rather than too few. As the researcher becomes more knowledgeable in the profession, he/she will become more skilled at quickly isolating the relevant facts.

In many cases, the basic issue has already been identified before the research process begins, e.g., when a client requests advice as to the proper handling of a specific transaction. However, further refinement of the exact issue is often required. This process of refining the issue at hand is referred to as *problem distillation*, whereby a general issue is restated in sufficiently specific terms. If the statement of the issue is too broad or general, the researcher is apt to waste valuable time consulting sources irrelevant to the specific issue.

Factors to consider in the identification and statement of the issue include: (1) the exact source of the issue, (2) justification for the issue, and (3) a determination of the scope of the issue. To successfully design and execute an investigation, the critical issue must be stated clearly and precisely. As explained in Chapter 6, many research tools, especially computerized databases, are indexed by a set of descriptive words. Since key words aid in reference identification, failure to describe the facts (the key words) in sufficient detail can cause one to overlook important sources. Undoubtedly, writing a clear, concise statement of the problem is the most important task in research. Failure to frame all the facts can, and often will, lead to an erroneous conclusion.

Collect Evidence.   As previously stated, problem-solving research cannot begin until the researcher defines the problem. Once the issue is adequately defined, the researcher is ready to proceed with step two of the research process, the collection of evidence. This step usually encompasses a detailed review of relevant authoritative accounting or auditing literature and a survey of present practice. In collecting evidence, the researcher should be familiar with the various sources available, which ones to use, which ones not to use, and the order in which these sources should be examined. This early identification of the relevant sources will aid in the efficient conduct of the research steps. A number of research tools that will aid in the collection of evidence are available and are discussed in detail in Chapters 4 through 6. In cases where authoritative literature does not exist on a specific issue, the accountant or auditor should develop a theoretical resolution of the issue based upon a logical analysis of the factors involved. In addition, the economic consequences of the various alternatives need to be evaluated in the development of a conclusion. It should also be noted that, in practice, normally a solution is not readily apparent. Professional judgment and theoretical analysis will be key elements in the research process.

Evaluate Results and Identify Alternatives. Once a thorough investigation and collection of evidence has been completed, the next step is to evaluate the results and identify alternatives to arrive at one or more tentative conclusions to the issue at hand. Each alternative should be supported fully by authoritative literature or a theoretical justification with complete and concise documentation. One cannot expect to draw sound conclusions from faulty information. Sound, documented conclusions can be drawn only when the information has been properly collected, organized, and interpreted.

Further analysis and research may be needed as to the appropriateness of the various alternatives identified. This reevaluation may require further discussions with the client or consultations with colleagues. In discussing an issue with a client, the researcher should be cognizant of the fact that management may not always be objective in evaluating alternatives. For example, the issue may involve the acceptability of an accounting method that is currently being used by the client. In such cases, the research is directed toward the support or rejection of an alternative already decided on by management. The possibility of bias should cause the researcher to retain a degree of skepticism in discussions with the client regarding a conclusion.

Develop Conclusion. After a detailed analysis of the alternatives, including economic consequences, the researcher develops a conclusion. The final conclusion selected from the alternatives identified should be documented thoroughly and be well supported by the evidence gathered. Then the conclusion is presented to the client as a proposed solution to the issue.

Communicate Results. The most important point in the communication of the conclusion, which often takes the form of a research memorandum, is that the words selected must be objective and unbiased. The memorandum should contain a clear statement of the issue researched, a statement of the facts, a brief and precise discussion of the issue, and a straightforward conclusion based upon supported and identified authoritative literature. The written communication should follow the conventional rules of grammar, spelling, and punctuation. Nothing diminishes credibility faster than misspellings, incorrect grammar, or misuse of words.

In drafting the memo, common errors to be avoided include excessive discussion of the issue and facts, which indicates that the memo has not been drafted with sufficient precision; excessive citations to authoritative sources— cite only the main support for the conclusion reached; and appearing to avoid a conclusion by pleading the need for additional facts. Novice researchers too often include information that was found to be wholly irrelevant to the issue at hand. The desire to include this information in the memorandum should be avoided since it often distracts from the current solution to the problem. Be careful and precise.

A serious weakness in any part of the research process threatens the worth of the entire research effort. Therefore, each segment of the process should be addressed with equal seriousness as to its impact on the entire research project.

Summary

The importance of research in the work of a practicing accountant or auditor should now be apparent. Few practitioners ever experience a work week that does not include the investigation and analysis of an accounting or auditing issue. Thus, every practicing accountant or auditor should possess the ability to conduct practical research in a systematic way. The goal of this text is to aid the practitioner in developing a basic framework, or methodology, to assist in the research process.

The emphasis of the following chapters is on applied or practical research that deals with solutions to immediate practical issues rather than pure or basic research that has little or no present-day application. Chapter 2 presents an overview of the importance of critical-thinking and effective writing skills that every researcher (accountant/auditor) must possess to be an effective professional. Chapters 3 and 4 provide an overview of the environment of accounting and auditing/ attestation research, with an emphasis on the standard-setting process. Also presented in these two chapters is the hierarchy of the authoritative literature that aids in determining where to start and end the research process. Chapter 5 presents a discussion of the sources of authoritative literature as well as an explanation of access techniques to the professional literature. Chapter 6 discusses other available research tools that may aid in the efficient and effective conduct of practical research, with an emphasis on computerized research via various databases. New to this edition of the text is a presentation on accounting and auditing research via the Internet—the information superhighway. In order to acquaint individuals not familiar with the Internet, a disk entitled "Getting Started on the Internet" has been enclosed with this text. This disk, the equivalent a 200-page book, informs the reader about the Internet system and how to access the Internet. Chapter 6 will also discuss how the accountant/auditor can use the Internet for accounting and auditing research. Chapter 7 presents the Disclosure software included on a second disk with the text; this software contains a sample of real company data from SEC-filed documents. Many practitioners use Disclosure in their daily research. Chapter 8 concludes with a refinement of the research process by presenting specific annotated procedures for conducting and documenting the research process via a comprehensive problem.

Discussion Questions

1. Define the term *research*.

2. Define *accounting* or *auditing* research.

3. Why is accounting or auditing research necessary?

4. What is the objective of accounting or auditing research?

5. What role does research play within an accounting firm or department? Who conducts the research?

6. What are the functions or responsibilities of the Policy Committee and Executive Subcommittee within a multioffice firm?

7. Identify and explain some basic questions the researcher must address in performing accounting and/or auditing research.

8. Differentiate between *pure* and *applied* research.

9. Identify the characteristics that a researcher (practitioner) should possess.

10. Distinguish between *a priori* and *a posteriori* research.

11. Explain the analogy of the California court decision dealing with legal research as it relates to the accounting/auditing practitioner.

12. Explain how the research process adds value to the services offered by an accounting firm.

13. What economic consequences are considered in the standards-setting process?

14. Compare and contrast the varying views of research.

15. Explain the five basic steps involved in the accounting or auditing research process.

16. Discuss how research can support or refute a biased alternative.

17. Explain what is meant by problem distillation and describe its importance in the research process.

18. Your conclusion to the research will often be presented to your boss or client in the form of a research memorandum. Identify the basic points that should be contained in this memo. Also identify some common errors that should be avoided in the drafting of the memo.

19. Explain the necessity of critical-thinking skills in the research process.

20. Why did the SEC bring an Enforcement action against a CPA concerning research?

CRITICAL THINKING AND EFFECTIVE WRITING

Learning Objectives

After completing this chapter, you should understand:

- The importance of "adding value" to the research process.

- How critical-thinking skills can help add this value.

- How competent writing forms a key element of critical-thinking skills.

- How to strengthen your writing skills.

Accounting professionals, whether in public accounting, management accounting, or not-for-profit accounting, provide value-added services to others in a dynamic, complex, expanding, and constantly changing profession. These professionals need to develop a paradigm of skills addressing "how to think" and also "how to write effectively." In other words, in today's complex financial world, accountants/auditors must develop lifelong learning skills to *think critically* (to grasp the meaning of complex concepts and principles), to judge and apply these concepts and principles to specific issues, and then to *communicate* the results *effectively* to others. This chapter will provide the accounting/audit researcher with some insights as to the development of these skills.

Critical Thinking

As the accounting profession continues to evolve into the role of a decision-making advisor, the accountant is being required to think more critically. Descriptors of critical thinking have been summarized as follows:

1. Critical thinking is nonalgorithmic. The path of an action is not fully specified in advance.
2. Critical thinking is often complex.
3. Critical thinking often yields multiple solutions rather than unique solutions that need to be analyzed with their respective costs and benefits.
4. Critical thinking involves making interpretations.
5. Critical thinking involves the application of multiple criteria.
6. Critical thinking involves uncertainty. One needs to tolerate ambiguity and uncertainty.
7. Critical thinking involves self-regulation of the thinking process.
8. Critical thinking involves imposing meaning, finding structure in apparent disorder.
9. Critical thinking is effortful. It entails considerable mental work of elaboration and judgment.[1]

The following sections provide some further insights in the development of these skills.

Critical Thinking: A Definition

The term *critical* is defined in the *American Heritage Dictionary* as "characterized by careful and exact evaluation and judgment." The word is not negative, nor is it neutral. "Critical thinking" points to a positive ability in those who

---

[1] Resnick, Lauren B., *Education and Learning to Think,* (Washington, D.C.: National Academy Press, 1987).

possess it. Critical thinking is a rational response to questions that cannot be answered definitively and for which all relevant information may be unavailable. Its purpose is to explore situations to arrive at optimal, justifiable hypotheses or conclusions. It rests on a basic *wariness*, a willingness to take nothing for granted, to approach each experience as if it were unique.

This approach is quite different from other methods of thinking. Ideas are always present in our minds; hence we are always "thinking" in one way or another. Daydreaming is one kind of thinking (usually an unfocused kind), as is remembering (focused but uncreative—simple information retrieval). But critical thinking is purposeful, goal-oriented, and creative—an active process rooted in a series of qualities that add up to the attitude we call *wariness,* taking nothing for granted.

It is an axiom among professional writers that good writing always results from intensive *rewriting*; critical thinking is basically *rethinking,* refusing the obvious and easy way. The qualities that lie behind rethinking include:

- A willingness to say "I don't know."
- An openness to alternative ways of seeing and doing—alternatives that are based on understanding how things work.
- An interest in the ideas of others that is shown by paying attention to them— even when they don't agree with yours.
- Thoughtfulness, or caring, that is shown by genuine curiosity, not just idle curiosity.
- A desire to find out what other people have done and thought.
- An insistence on getting the best evidence before you make up your mind.
- An openness to your own intuition.[2]

The purpose of critical thinking is always the same—to understand. But the goal goes beyond the purpose: critical thinking almost invariably leads to evaluation and therefore to judgment. In the end, you will judge the value of that which you have reflected on.

An Outline of Critical Thinking

The difficulty in discussing critical thinking concisely springs from two characteristics of critical thinking itself, as Boostrom explains:

> First, clear thinking results less from practicing skills than from adopting such attitudes as persistence, open-mindedness, thoroughness, and flexibility. . . . Second, thinking is not a single

---

2   Boostrom, Robert, *Developing Creative and Critical Thinking : An Integrated Approach,* (Chicago: National Textbook Co., 1992), pp. 24–25.

process that can be divided into a series of steps. Instead, it is a family of processes that enlighten and support each other.[3]

It is this complexity that Harold Bloom was attempting to analyze and define when in 1956 he published his taxonomic table of kinds of thought. An example is presented in Figure 2-1.

In the nineteenth century, Oliver Wendell Holmes spoke of one-story, two-story, and three-story people: The one-storied were fact-collectors with no aims beyond the facts; the two-storied were able to compare, reason, and generalize using the results of the fact-collectors' labors; the three-storied individuals could idealize, imagine, and predict. In our own day, the Illinois Renewal Institute has posited three levels of thought. The lowest level is *recall,* in which one defines, describes, lists, recites, and selects. The second level is *process,* in which one compares, contrasts, classifies, sorts, distinguishes, explains, infers, sequences, analyzes, synthesizes, and analogizes. The third level is *application,* in which one evaluates, generalizes, imagines, judges, predicts, speculates, hypothesizes, and forecasts. Useful as this scheme may be, Bloom's taxonomy remains the most detailed and the most widely accepted.

Bloom's taxonomy implies that the levels of thinking are incremental: one must be able to perform at level four, for example, before moving up to level five. (The ideal reader, writer, accountant, or auditor moves up the levels until he or she can perform at the top level.) To exercise the level six skills, one must already possess the skills below that level. To be able to *infer* properly, for example, one must often be able first to define and describe accurately the objects or situations from which one will infer. The skills increase in complexity as the level rises. To analyze a situation, for example, is a far more complicated process than simply to recall a situation, while to evaluate a situation (using definite criteria and for a given purpose) is more complicated than both analyzing or recalling. It can be argued that the basic differences between the levels are largely a matter of attitude, not procedure. That is, the ability to progress up through the levels depends, first, on one's ability to internalize the qualities we noted on page 18. Secondly, to move up depends on the ability to make certain specific decisions, which are listed below.

The Elements of Critical Thinking

The following list of decisions is freely adapted from a longer list by Robert H. Ennis.[4]

1. Deciding on the meaning of a statement.

---

3 *Ibid.,* p.1, Teacher's Manual.

4 Ennis, Robert H., "A Concept of Critical Thinking," *Harvard Educational Review,* Vol. 32, No. 1 (Winter, 1962), pp. 81–111.

FIGURE 2-1   Example of Applying and Understanding Bloom's Taxonomy

Level No.	Major Categories in Bloom's Taxonomy	Illustrative General Instructional Objectives	Illustrative Behavioral Terms for Stating Specific Learned Outcomes
1.	**Knowledge** represents recalling previously learned materials.	Knows common terms, specific facts, basic concepts and principles.	Defines, describes, labels, lists, reproduces, selects, and states.
2.	**Comprehension** involves "grasping" the material, including translating words into numbers, summarizing or interpreting the materials, and estimating future trends.	Understands facts and principles; translates verbal materials into mathematical formulas; estimates future consequences implied in the data; and justifies methods and procedures.	Converts, defends, distinguishes, estimates, extends, explains, predicts, rewrites, and summarizes.
3.	**Application** of the use of previously learned materials into new situations.	(Correctly) applies laws and theories into new and practical situations.	Changes, computes, demonstrates, discovers, manipulates, modifies, shows, solves, and uses.
4.	**Analysis** breaks down the material into its component parts to understand better its organizational structure.	Recognizes unstated assumptions and logical gaps in reasoning; distinguishes between facts and inferences; and evaluates the relevancy of data.	Breaks down, diagrams, differentiates, discriminates, distinguishes, infers, outlines, selects, relates, separates, and subdivides.
5.	**Synthesis** puts parts together to form a new whole, usually involving creative behaviors and new patterns or structures (e.g., developing a new schema for classifying information).	Writes a well-organized research paper; gives a well-organized speech; integrate learning from different areas into a new plan to solve a problem; and formulates a new schema to classify objects or events.	Categorizes, combines, compiles, composes, creates, devises, assigns, explains, generates, recognizes, plans, revises, reorganizes, rewrites, tells, or writes.

FIGURE 2-1 (continued)

Level No.	Major Categories in Bloom's Taxonomy	Illustrative General Instructional Objectives	Illustrative Behavioral Terms for Stating Specific Learned Outcomes
6.	**Evaluation** judges the value of the statement (based upon definite criteria) for a given purpose. The criteria can be internal (organization) or external (relevant to the given purpose).	Judges the logical consistency of the presented material, how well the data "support" the "conclusions," and how well the end product adheres to the internal and external criteria.	Appraises, compares, concludes, criticizes, contrasts, explains, justifies, interprets, relates, summarizes, and supports.

At a low level, grasping the meaning of a statement involves simply not mistaking the intent of a statement; the evidence of this is the ability to put the statement into one's own words without significantly altering the meaning. But as one moves up the levels, the skill changes. For example, the formula (the statement) for determining the sum of an arithmetic series of numbers is this:

$$(n+1) \times (n/2)$$

Being able to recall the formula (one level) and apply it (a higher level) does not demonstrate that one knows what the statement means. The statement means that the sum of each of the pairs that can be made in the series multiplied by the number of pairs yields the sum of the whole series.[5] Deriving that meaning takes a higher order of reading skill than simple paraphrase. In any case, grasping the meaning of a statement implies that one knows the application of the statement in a situation and can recognize statements that contradict or support it. This concept forms the basis of all the other logical aspects, each differing only in the particular phase of the entire realm of critical thinking. In accounting and auditing research, a clear and concise meaning of the issue is essential to effective research.

2. Deciding whether a conclusion follows necessarily from the underlying data. Only deductive reasoning yields "necessary" conclusions. "A conclusion follows necessarily if its denial contradicts the assertion of the premises,"[6] and from this one criterion come all the rules of deductive reasoning, whether it is

---

5   *Ibid.*, p. 96.

6   *Ibid.*, p. 87.

mathematical reasoning, "if-then" reasoning, or syllogistic reasoning. For example, an auditor must ascertain that the client's accounts receivable balance is both reasonable and collectible before rendering an audit opinion on the (entire) financial statements. This process requires applying generally accepted auditing standards, which, in turn, often rely heavily upon deductive logic.

3. Deciding whether an observation statement is reliable. Ennis provides what he calls a "combined list of principles from the fields of law, history, and science" that deal with the reliability of observation statements:

> Observation statements tend to be more reliable if the observer:
> - Was unemotional, alert, and disinterested.
> - Was skilled at observing the sort of thing observed.
> - Had sensory equipment that was in good condition.
> - Has a reputation for veracity.
> - Used precise technique.
> - Had no preconception about the way the observation turned out.

> Observation statements tend to be more reliable if the observation conditions:
> - Were such that the observer had good access.
> - Provided a satisfactory medium of observation.

> Observation statements tend to be more reliable to the extent that the statement:
> - Is close to being a statement of direct observation.
> - Is corroborated.
> - Is corroboratable.
> - Comes from a disinterested source with a reputation for veracity.

> Observation statements, if based on a record, tend to be more reliable if the record:
> - Was made at the time of observation.
> - Was made by the person making the statement.
> - Is believed by the person making the statement to be correct.

> Observation statements tend to be more reliable than inferences made from them.[7]

In an audit environment, auditors should apply this taxonomy in gathering and evaluating audit evidence. For example, in general it is assumed that externally generated data is more reliable than data derived from internal sources (e.g., bank or other third-party confirmations are a more reliable source of evidence than internal bank reconciliations, correspondence files, or general ledger detail).

4. Deciding whether an inductive conclusion is warranted.

---

7   *Ibid.*, p. 90.

An inductive conclusion is an inference, a probable (but not certain) conclusion drawn from two or more premises. An inductive conclusion can be tested by asking oneself (1) Are the premises reliable? and (2) If the premises are reliable, is the conclusion convincing? Premises can be judged by whether the evidence that went into their making meets a series of criteria:

1. Sufficient: Does the accountant have adequate evidence to reach a proper conclusion or should further questions be asked?
2. Representative: Is the evidence provided objective?
3. Relevant: Does the evidence relate directly to the provided assertion?
4. Accurate: Does the evidence come from reliable primary or secondary sources?

Often the researcher conducting accounting research will be gathering evidence from primary and secondary accounting sources, as explained in Chapter 3.

5. Deciding whether a statement is an assumption.

In one sense, an assumption is simply a presupposition. "The Army's lack of planning caused unnecessary casualties" assumes that the Army did not plan. In such an argument, the lack of planning cannot be assumed but must be proved. In another sense, an assumption is simply a statement that the conclusion follows and depends upon. Such assumptions are checked by deciding if they are plausible and simpler than the alternatives, necessary (in empirical situations) to whatever action or event is posited, and acceptable to experts. For example, auditors spend much of their time assessing the validity of many client assumptions, including the adequacy of the allowance for doubtful accounts and the expected lives of depreciable assets.

6. Deciding whether a definition is adequate.

Persuasive definitions—those that judge a concept, as in "'liberal' means 'standing up for the right to choose'"—are always suspect in critical thinking. Beyond persuasion, the criterion is simply, "Is this definition good enough for our purposes in this situation?" Auditors generally consider the concepts of materiality and audit risk for a client's assertion in ascertaining the sufficiency of the evidence, recognizing that the more evidence the auditor accumulates, the lower the risk of misstatement.

7. Deciding whether a statement made by an alleged authority is acceptable.

There are really two questions here: Is the source an authority? Is the statement acceptable? An authority, as Ennis states, is someone who makes statements in his or her field, has studied the matter, has a good reputation, is disinterested and in full possession of his or her faculties, has followed accepted procedures in reaching conclusions, and is aware that his or her reputation could be affected by the statements that are made. Whether the statements are acceptable depends on accepting the person as an authority and then checking the specific statements by reference to our other six principles. Auditors often rely on authorities—especially to help satisfy the valuation assertion (e.g., using qualified appraisers to help valuate precious gems); however, the auditor should ascertain the competence, independence, and "expected reasonableness" of this authority in ascertaining how much reliance to place on the conclusions the authority gives. Also, as explained in subsequent chapters of this text, the accounting profession has developed a hierarchy of authoritative accounting and auditing pronouncements that is utilized in the research process.

Making these decisions is critical thinking. As Boostrom states, in critical thinking "you decide first what the words mean, then whether they make sense, and finally whether you believe them."[8]

Goldratt's[9] best-selling business book, *The Goal,* provides yet another example of using critical-thinking skills in a business organization. He describes a company that has "floundered," because it conducted its business under certain constant, time-honored assumptions as:

1. Keep all employees busy all of the time.
2. Order materials in the largest quantities possible to receive the lowest price.
3. Keep the manufacturing robots working all the time (to minimize "downtime").
4. Measure the "cost" of an idle machine as its depreciation expense.
5. Allow management to change the priority of jobs in process to meet customs "pressure."

Goldratt demonstrates that the company could operate much more profitably by "challenging" these assumptions (i.e., by using higher-order critical-thinking skills), thereby yielding dramatically improved results. He shows that adhering to these "old" policies slowed efficiency rather than enhancing it. His new approach includes:

1. Since "busy" employees producing unneeded inventory waste resources, the company should ask certain production employees to perform quality control and preventative maintenance procedures rather than produce "non-essential" parts.
2. Since "large" materials orders can increase inventory unnecessarily, the company should order smaller quantities of parts inventory.
3. Since robots, like employees, only increase unneeded inventory, the company should consider the cost of the inventory they produce in deciding whether to allow the robots to work.

---

8   Boostrom, *op. cit.,* p. 198.

9   Goldratt, Eliyahu M., *The Goal,* (New Haven, Conn.: North River Press, 1992).

4. Since "bottlenecks" often prevent a factory from working to its full potential, the company should focus on reducing such operate bottleneck constraints.
5. Since a "rush" environment generally impairs the optimal timing of the production process, the company should not alter the normal work flow for "special" jobs.

Based upon the above discussion, accountants/auditors should develop and utilize critical-thinking skills to add value to their services, an important task for all professionals—including newly hired employees. A summary of some necessary basic critical-thinking skills appears in Figure 2-2.

Effective Writing

The ability to communicate effectively, both orally and in writing, is essential for success as a professional accountant. Good communication skills are emphasized in the following personal anecdotes as shared by two business professionals:

FIGURE 2-2 Basic Critical-Thinking Skills

SKILL	DESCRIPTION
Value Added Services	Advise, predict, detect, recommend, and evaluate.
Wariness	Take nothing for granted. Approach each experience as a "unique" event.
Rethinking	Do not perform tasks in an obvious and routine manner. Use innovative, alternative ways to perform the necessary jobs. Insist on obtaining the "best" available evidence—considering the related costs.
Evaluation and Judgment	Use definitive criteria to obtain the goal of the assignment; then apply reasonable judgment after this evaluation.
Incremental Levels of Thinking	Apply "lower" levels of thinking before progressing to "higher" levels.

Dennis R. Beresford, Chairman, Financial Accounting Standards Board:

In accounting and all other professions, we must have the appropriate technical skills. But if we cannot communicate what we know, the value of technical skills is lessened. For example, knowing how to compute corporate income taxes is a valuable skill. Being able to tell others how to do it magnifies the value of that technical skill. Others can capitalize on your knowledge only if you can communicate it.

Hugh B. Jacks, President, BellSouth Services:

Learning to communicate well should be a top priority for anyone aspiring to lead or advance in a career. Strong technical skills are needed, but technical ability alone will not result in career advancement. Those who develop only technical skills always will work for people who have both technical and leadership abilities, and communication is the key ingredient in leadership.[10]

One popular view of the relationship between thinking and writing is that first one determines what it is one wants to say (thinking) and then one sets these ideas down (writing). That's a misconception, but like many popular misconceptions, there is a grain of truth in it: we need to have some idea of where we are going before we begin a draft. But we don't carry the draft in memory to then put it into language. After all, we think in language; hence the difference between thinking and writing is not so great as we might imagine. In addition, writing is not just a matter of putting down a complete draft; it involves putting down isolated ideas, writing reminders to ourselves, making outlines, charting different sides of an issue. We usually write based on some form of which has already been written, not from pure thought.

If thinking and writing are intimately related, it follows that critical thinking and effective writing are also. Effective writing is not just a matter of form but of content—the phrase *garbage in, garbage out* applies to more than computers. One must think critically in order to write effectively.

Writing as a Process

Writing is a way to make meaning of our experiences—in other words, it is a form of learning, and occurs as a complicated chain of processes. The complication stems from the fact that writers do many things at the same time: They remember past experience (including their reading) while they plan what they intend to write (from the next word to the total document); they try to convey large concepts

---

10 Himstreet, William C., Wayne M. Baty, and Carol M. Lehman, *Business Communications,* (Dallas: Wadsworth Publishing Co., 1993), p. xxxiv.

while at the same time supplying supporting evidence and details; they consider what they know while they consider what the audience needs to know for its unique purposes; and they continually change their minds and revise while they try to keep their main focus, their central idea and purpose, in mind and in the text.

Perhaps the best way to bring some order to the subject is to envision first the intended, final product. The AICPA defines effective writing *in essay answers for the CPA examination* as a series of document characteristics:

1. *Coherent organization.* Responses should be organized so that the ideas are arranged logically and the flow of thought is easy to follow. Generally, knowledge is best expressed by using short paragraphs composed of short sentences. Moreover, short paragraphs, each limited to the development of one principal idea, can better emphasize the main points in the answer. Each principal idea should be placed in the first sentence of the paragraph, followed by supporting concepts and examples.

2. *Conciseness.* Conciseness requires that candidates present complete thoughts in as few words as possible, while ensuring that important points are covered adequately. Short sentences and simple wording also contribute to concise writing.

3. *Clarity.* A clearly written response prevents uncertainty concerning the candidate's meaning or reasoning. Clarity involves using words with specific and precise meaning, including proper technical terminology. Well-constructed sentences also contribute to clarity.

4. *Use of standard English.* Standard English is characterized by exacting standards of punctuation and capitalization, accurate spelling, exact diction, an expressive vocabulary, and knowledgeable usage choices.

5. *Responsiveness to the requirements of the question.* Answers should directly address the requirements of the question and demonstrate the candidate's awareness of the purpose of the writing task. Responses should not be broad expositions on the general subject matter.

6. *Appropriateness for the reader.* Writing that is appropriate for the reader takes into account the reader's background, knowledge of the subject, interests, and concerns. The requirements of some essay questions may ask candidates to prepare a written document for a certain reader, such as an engagement memorandum for a CPA's client. When the intended reader is not specified, the candidate should assume the intended reader is a knowledgeable CPA.[11]

It seems fair to assume that any professional accountant should apply the same criteria to his/her writing as suggested by the AICPA. So let us inspect these six criteria.

Of the six characteristics, three are linked to *editing* skills and three to *composing* skills. (Composing is what one does before and during the actual drafting of a paper; editing is what one does to the draft.) The editing components are

---

11 Examinations Division, AICPA, *Report of the Testing of Writing Skills Subtask Force of the CPA Examination Change Implementation Task Force,* September 18, 1990.

conciseness, clarity, and the use of standard English. All three of these are largely matters of rewriting. That is, writers (except under unreasonable time restraints, as in some poorly timed examinations) should not trouble themselves about conciseness, clarity, and standard English in a first draft; it is only confusing and self-defeating to attempt too many tasks at once.

The three composing components are coherent organization, responsiveness to the requirements of the question, and appropriateness for the reader. That is, these three elements must be taken into consideration and dealt with before commencing the first draft. That is not to say that changes relative to these three elements will not be made in revision, but one cannot write a focused first draft without dealing with these elements first.

Composing Elements

Organization. Let us begin by considering coherent organization. Before one can organize, there must be something to organize. Material to organize results from information retrieval that is directed to answering a specific question. In other words, effective writing begins with a question; the efficient writer begins not with a topic or a problem but a question that he or she wants the paper to answer. Often the question is supplied by the client or the situation: Where can the client get the best after-tax return on investment? Which of the branches is the one to sell off? What's the best way to report unexpected earnings? A question helps focus the research that the writer must conduct; a topic opens up vast reaches of information retrieval. So the first step is to ask a specific question.

Because this text deals with the "how to" of retrieving important and relevant information in other chapters, we will not discuss gathering information here but will assume that it has been gathered. Now comes the task of evaluating the information—using critical-thinking skills—and of coming to a general answer to the question that was posed. Perhaps at this point the writer can't come up with a definite answer—the answer will evolve as the writer proceeds. More often than not, a general answer will appear by the time the writer reads through the information several times. In any case, the answer is used to determine what material will go into the paper. Organizing material is not just a matter of putting shape into the information gathered but of organizing material that is now seen to be important and relevant to the answer and to the audience's specific needs.

This process is much easier if one commits each step to paper, even if it's only informal notes. It is a good idea to write down the answer to the question— in whatever rough form it surfaces. Often when writing down the answer—let's call it a focus—the writer unconsciously discovers or invents his or her organization. For example, suppose a client is asking which state, Michigan or Florida, would be the best for her to establish residency in, from an economic standpoint. Suppose that after examining the issues of state income taxes, sales and property taxes, unemployment/welfare taxes, municipal and inheritance taxes, and the cost of food, clothing, and shelter, one decides that Florida is the better choice because the tax advantages more than outweigh the higher prices for food, clothing, and shelter. If the answer, the focus, is "Mrs. X would benefit more financially by establishing residency in Florida than in Michigan . . . ," the writer will then begin to spell out reasons: ". . . because the tax advantages far outweigh the higher costs of food, clothing, and shelter." Part of the answer—perhaps most of it—is now organized: the writer will discuss the tax advantages, one by one; then present the costs of food, clothing, and shelter; and then move to a conclusion showing the difference that favors Florida.

The pattern of organization should be selected before the first draft is written. There are really only four basic patterns of organization. Rhetoricians call them *modes:*

1. *The descriptive mode.* Description, whether physical or conceptual, moves from the whole to the part or the part to the whole. A student facing a question about the economic causes of the American Civil War may opt for a descriptive organization with a focus that forecasts that pattern: "There were three major economic causes of the American Civil War: the struggle for control of the textile trade, the battle for the British markets, and the cost of slavery." The whole (economic causes) has been broken down into its parts.
2. *The narrative mode.* Narrative arranges objects or events in a sequence in time, usually chronological. The simplest pattern here is a chronological sequence without flashbacks for explanation. *Cause and effect* is a narrative arrangement that emphasizes the causal relationship between one part of the chronology and another. *Process* is a narrative arrangement that emphasizes repeated and repeatable chronological sequences.
3. *The classification mode.* Classification puts an object or event into a larger group, defines the group, and shows how the subject shares features with the group (or perhaps how it differs): Classification can be used as a kind of definition.
4. *The evaluation mode.* Evaluation consists of (a) setting standards or criteria by which something can be judged; (b) relating the subject to the criteria to show how it meets or does not meet the criteria; and (c) drawing the conclusion that follows. All patterns of organization are members of these four modes, which are, of course, not artificial designs but *modes of thought;* they imitate patterns of human thinking. The writer needs to be consistent in following one pattern; shifts confuse the reader.

Responsiveness.   The second composing element in the AICPA list is "Responsiveness to the requirements of the question." In fact, except for reasons of emphasis, this item could have been collapsed into the first composing element, "Coherent organization," or into the last, "Appropriateness for the reader." A paper should never attempt to incorporate all that a writer knows about the subject because the answer the writer gives should include only material that is relevant and important to the issue (and therefore determining what is responsive is part of the process of determining what should be included at the early stage of selecting material for organization) and/or specific to the needs of the reader. Most readers don't need or want to hear about the writer's discovery process; they want the results of the process. Generally, they want application, not theory. If the writer carefully selects material by using the answer and the knowledge of the audience's needs as a selecting device, the question of responsiveness will evolve on its own. For example, a staff accountant would omit more detail in preparing a report for a subordinate than for a superior.

Appropriateness.   The third composing element is "Appropriateness for the reader." It is important that the writer know the level and type of experience the reader has had with the subject so that one does not write "down" to the reader or overestimate the reader's knowledge. Furthermore, the writer will profit from knowing what values the reader has that relate to the subject so that one does not offend unknowingly. The reader's experience, level of knowledge, and attitude toward the subject help to determine what the writer says. For example, a tax specialist would use different degrees of technical jargon in composing a memorandum to describe a highly technical tax issue for a client, for a subordinate, or for a superior.

Once the writer has a plan of organization, a rough list of the materials to be included, and a profile of the reader in mind, it is time to draft the first version. The first draft should be done without regard for mechanics (spelling, punctuation, grammar, usage); the important thing is to get the important and relevant information on paper in organized form. Once the draft is completed, it can be edited.

Editing Elements

If we use the AICPA list as a guide, editing is a matter of polishing the prose so that it possesses conciseness, clarity, and standard English.

Conciseness.   A concise paper contains no extraneous matter and does not repeat itself. Hence the first editorial sweep should be for unity and coherence: that is, the writer looks for ideas, examples, or facts that wander beyond the boundaries set by the focus—and then removes that dross. (It is then proper to ask oneself whether the paper now has *sufficient* material.) Accountants/auditors can best make their writing concise by eliminating unnecessary words. Writing should be like a machine: the fewer parts necessary to make it run smoothly the better. For example, an accountant can reduce a 14-word statement: "We hope the entire staff will assist us in our efforts to reduce costs," to ten words: "We hope the entire staff will help us reduce costs." The second sweep should be for coherence: Does the paper follow the organizational plan? Do the pieces fit together and flow properly?

Clarity. A clear paper has made the right word choices (diction) and has chosen the most effective sentence patterns (syntax). Such choices have been made much easier by currently available software. Computer-based style checkers such as *RightWriter* or one of the *Grammatik* series can identify probable trouble spots: overuse of the passive voice, long or esoteric words, and sentence fragments. In the end, the writer, of course, must judge what is proper and effective—the style checker only warns. Furthermore, style checkers generally cannot detect dangling modifiers, squinting modifiers, or lapses in subject-verb or pronoun-antecedent agreement. Style checkers are usually helpers, but they are not solutions.

Precision forms an additional important element of clear writing. That is, the meaning of the sentence must be clear. An example of poor diction may be: "While wearing a new three-piece suit, I was unable to detect the cause of the client's decline in revenues and became worrisome." This statement contains several "problems," including:

1. Who was wearing the three-piece suit—the client or the accountant?
2. Why make mention of the suit at all, since it bears little relationship to the accounting problem?
3. Who was being worrisome—the client or the accountant?
4. Is "worrisome" a proper term to use?

A revised, more precise version of this sentence might be: "I became worried about being unable to detect the cause of the client's decline in revenues."

Business writing suffers generally from inflation, as if business writers were secretly afraid that what they have to say is not important enough to be said plainly. Inflation produces confusion and misunderstanding, which in turn causes anger and separation between writer and reader, exactly the opposite of what business writing intends. Moreover, it is expensive, since inflated writing takes longer to read and understand and often is misunderstood.

One kind of inflation is the overuse of prepositional phrases, facilitated by using some form of the verb *to be*. Here are two actual sentences from a business report, quoted by Richard Lanham in *Revising Business Prose:*

> Normal belief is that the preparation and submission of a proposal in response to a Request for Proposal (RFP), Request for Quotation (RFQ), or a bid in response to an Invitation for Bids (IFB) is no different than that of an unsolicited proposal for a grant from the National Science Foundation or another government agency; and that if such a proposal or bid is hand-delivered to the Office of Extramural Support on a Friday afternoon, it will get mailed the same day to reach Washington, D.C. by 4:00 p.m. of the following Monday. Having read this article, however, the reader, we hope, will agree that this

is an erroneous belief which has led and, if continued to be believed, will lead to unhappy experiences for all concerned.[12]

A more precise rewriting and meaning is as follows:

Unsolicited grant proposals differ from ones solicited by a Request for Proposal (RFP), a Request for Quotation (RFQ), or an Invitation for Bids (IFB). If you bring a solicited proposal to our office on Friday afternoon, thinking it will be mailed that day and reach Washington by Monday at 4:00 p.m, you will be disappointed. We hope this article has shown you why.[13]

The effective writer strives for economy and, therefore, for clarity.

Standard English.   The use of standard English, by which the AICPA means both usage (which is discussed above) and mechanical exactness, has also been made easier by software. Writers should run their drafts through a spell checker, without depending entirely on it: spell checkers will not pick up omitted words, nor do they know the difference between "their" and "there" and other homonyms. But they are invaluable in picking up simple misspellings, typographical errors, and doubled words. There are punctuation checkers available, but at this writing they are too primitive to be dependable. The writer, therefore, needs to reread carefully for punctuation errors; a good handbook is a helpful companion in this kind of editing. Some basic suggestions for word selection and sentence structure for effective writing are presented in Figure 2-3.

FIGURE 2-3   Word Selection and Sentence Structure Guidelines

1.   Visualize the reader in your word selection by using familiar words.
2.   Use the active voice in your writing.
3.   Choose short words.
4.   Use technical words and acronyms cautiously.
5.   Select your words for precise meanings.
6.   Limit your sentence content. Use short sentences.
7.   Use proper punctuation in sentence development
8.   Arrange your sentences for clarity and unity.

---

12 Lanham, Richard, *Revising Business Prose*, (New York: Charles Scribner's Sons, 1981), p. 1.

13 *Ibid.*, p. 6.

Success in critical thinking and effective writing comes from lifelong learning. The skills come with experience and practice, when the endeavors are taken seriously and when the professional realizes how intimately the two are related. Research that is not properly thought through and evaluated is useless; conclusions that are not communicated are lost. Moreover, there are dimensions to "satisfying the client" that often go unremarked. Richard Lanham writes that "this is why we worry so much about bad writing. It signifies incoherent people, failed social relationships."[14]

Critical thinking and effective writing are essential tools in accounting and auditing research. A summary table of some elements of effective writing is presented in Figure 2-4. In conclusion, accountants/auditors should focus on developing effective writing skills to enhance their everyday practice. The concepts outlined in this chapter will be exemplified throughout the remainder of this text.

FIGURE 2-4 Key Points of Effective Writing

Content	Effective writing should contain relevant, "value added" content matter, a process enhanced by using critical-thinking skills.
Chain of Processes	To add meaning from our experiences, convey "large" concepts, while supplying supporting evidence to these ideas.
Coherent Organization	Organize ideas logically, making the flow of thought easy to follow.
Conciseness	Use as few words as necessary to convey complete thoughts.
Clarity	Select effective words to state ideas with certainty.
Use of Standard English	Use appropriate punctuation and grammar, perhaps with the help of a computer-based spell/grammar checker.
Responsiveness	Ascertain that the answers directly address the research question.
Appropriateness for the Reader	Written communication should consider the intended reader's background and experience.

---

14 Ibid., p. 10.

Discussion Questions

1. Define *critical thinking.*

2. Describe the highest level of thinking according to Bloom's taxonomy.

3. Discuss what *grasping the meaning of a statement* implies.

4. What kind of statement or reasoning yields a necessary conclusion?

5. List some of the characteristics of a reliable observation statement.

6. Discuss how one tests an inductive conclusion.

7. Distinguish between the two meanings of *assumption.*

8. Give an example of a persuasive definition.

9. Define an authority.

10. Discuss the AICPA list of effective writing characteristics. Is it complete?

11. What are the four basic modes of thought that issue into organizational patterns?

12. What does a writer need to know about the reader?

13. What do *unity* and *coherence* mean when applied to a piece of writing?

14. Discuss the problem of *inflation* in business prose.

C H A P T E R   3

THE ENVIRONMENT OF ACCOUNTING RESEARCH

Learning Objectives

After completing this chapter, you should understand:

- The environment of accounting research.
- The bodies that set accounting standards.
- The process of standard setting.
- The types of authoritative pronouncements.
- The meaning of GAAP.
- The hierarchy of GAAP.
- The hierarchy of SEC publications.
- The current status of international accounting.

Research on an accounting issue is always conducted in a dynamic environment, since new professional standards are constantly being issued and existing standards updated or deleted. Of major significance is the fact that the researcher needs to be aware that in researching an issue, one needs to use the most recent authoritative pronouncement. The development of accounting standards is influenced by:

1. The requirements of federal, state, and local governments, and other regulatory bodies.
2. The influence of various tax laws on the financial reporting process.
3. The practices or problems of certain specialized industries, such as the motion picture or the oil and gas industries.
4. Inconsistencies in practice.
5. Disagreements among accountants, business executives, and others as to the objectives of financial statements.
6. The influence of professional organizations.

Figure 3-1 illustrates the complex environment into which the accounting practitioner/researcher must venture in pursuing the solution to a problem. Within this setting are resources containing numerous accounting standards, rules, and recommended practices. Yet, with so many directions in which to turn for guidance and with the need to solve the dilemma efficiently, the accountant must have a basic understanding of when and how these resources apply. The accountant must know not only where to find the generally accepted accounting principles and the established exceptions that are pertinent to the question at hand but, also, who speaks with the greatest authority within that context.

This chapter concentrates on the standard-setting process in accounting including the process conducted by the private sector (Financial Accounting Standards Board—FASB) and its predecessors, the public sector (U.S. Securities and Exchange Commission—SEC), as well as international dimensions.

Two questions are emphasized:

1. What constitutes generally accepted accounting principles (GAAP)?
2. What is the hierarchy of authoritative support? That is, which bodies speak with the loudest voices?

Standard-Setting Environment

Accounting standards have emerged over time to meet the needs of financial statement users. The number of users—primarily investors, lenders, and governmental entities—has increased enormously over the past 75 years, and the complexity of the business enterprise has increased with it. The result has been greater demand by users for more uniformity in accounting procedures to make

FIGURE 3-1   Accounting Research Environment

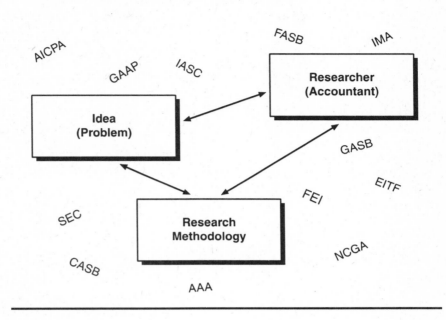

comparison of financial statements easier. Government agencies, legislative bodies, and professional organizations have responded to this demand.

Accounting Standard-Setting Process

Currently, the Financial Accounting Standards Board (FASB) is responsible for setting accounting standards in the private sector, just as the Governmental Accounting Standards Board (GASB) is for the public sector. Before 1973, the American Institute of Certified Public Accountants (AICPA) set standards for both sectors. Following is a brief historical perspective of the accounting standard-setting process.

American Institute of Certified Public Accountants.   In 1887, 31 accountants formed the American Association of Public Accountants (AAPA), the ancestor of the AICPA and the first national organization of accountants in the U.S. The chief purpose of the AAPA was to attest to the competency and integrity of its members. Until the turn of the century, U.S. audits were patterned after their British counterparts, with detailed scrutinizing of balance sheet audits. In

1917, at the request of the Federal Trade Commission, the transformed AAPA, under its new name, the American Institute of Accountants (AIA), prepared the first authoritative pronouncement, entitled *Balance-Sheet Audits.*

From 1939 to 1959 the AICPA and its predecessor, the AIA, through its Committee on Accounting Procedures (CAP), published 51 Accounting Research Bulletins (ARBs) dealing with a wide spectrum of accounting issues. In 1959, the newly created Accounting Principles Board (APB), which replaced the CAP, issued two major series of publications, the first—a set of 31 APB Opinions— now binding on all CPAs. Then in 1984, the Institute required that departures from APB Opinions (APBOs) be disclosed either in the notes to financial statements or in the audit reports of AICPA members in their capacity as independent auditors. CPAs could not give their approval to financial statements that deviated from APB Opinions unless they wanted to assume the considerable personal risk and burden of proof of defending the "unauthorized practices." Because few business enterprises or auditors were anxious to assume the burden of defending financial statements that differed from APB Opinions, this action gave new strength and authority to those Opinions. The APB also issued four nonauthoritative *Statements* (which addressed broad concepts rather than specific accounting principles) and several unofficial interpretations.

Before the establishment of the FASB in 1973, the AICPA was the recognized standard-setting body for the private sector. During that time the AICPA recognized the National Council on Governmental Accounting (NCGA, the standard-setting body of the Governmental Finance Officers Association) as an authoritative rule-making body for governmental entities. Other governmental organizations, including the Securities and Exchange Commission (SEC), the Internal Revenue Service (IRS), and the Cost Accounting Standards Board (CASB), also set certain accounting standards for entities in their domain.

Following formation of the FASB, the AICPA created an Accounting Standards Division to influence the development of accounting standards. The Accounting Standards Executive Committee (AcSEC) of the Accounting Standards Division issues *Statements of Position* (SOPs) to propose revisions of AICPA-published Industry Audit Guides and Accounting Guides. These SOPs do not establish enforceable accounting standards; however, members of the AICPA must justify departures from practices recommended in the SOPs. In addition, the Accounting Standards Division prepares *Issues Papers* to develop financial accounting and reporting issues that the division believes should be considered by the FASB.

Thus, AcSEC has become the spokesperson for the AICPA on financial accounting matters. It responds, for example, to FASB and SEC accounting pronouncements by issuing Comment Letters, Issue Letters, and SOPs, which the FASB may convert into *Statements of Financial Accounting Standards* (SFASs). It also often publishes brief notes and news releases in the AICPA's bi-weekly publication, *The CPA Letter,* reaching more than 300,000 members.

Various committees of the AICPA also publish *Accounting Research Monographs, Accounting Trends and Techniques*, and the *Accounting & Tax Index*, which are discussed in Chapter 6. The annual *Accounting Trends and Techniques* summarizes the accounting practices of 600 publicly owned companies. It presents tabulations of the numbers of surveyed companies that use particular practices; it also presents excerpts of actual reports issued by the surveyed companies.

The AICPA's Technical Information Service.   The Technical Information Service (TIS), one of the Institute's most valuable services, provides answers to any accounting or auditing question (except on tax or legal matters) posed by members. To`confer with a staff person, members can call toll-free 1-800-223-4158 (except in New York State, where the number is 1-800-522-5430), Monday through Friday from 9 A.M.–5 P.M. EST. The Institute receives some 14,000 queries a year and publishes the answers to the most frequently asked questions in *The Journal of Accountancy* and the Technical Practice Aids looseleaf services.

The Institute's library contains the largest collection of accounting information in the country. The library:

1. Makes bibliographies and articles available (except on tax or "in-depth" matters).
2. Charges only nominal copying and postage fees.
3. Provides information on almost any topic that appears in the *Accounting & Tax Index*.
4. Is available to AICPA members by phone, by mail, or in person. Members can call toll free 1-800-223-4155 (or in New York State, 1-800-522-5434), Monday and Wednesday through Friday from 9 A.M.–5 P.M. EST, and Tuesday from 10 A.M.–5 P.M. EST.

Financial Accounting Standards Board.   In 1972 the Wheat Committee (an AICPA committee) proposed that professional accounting standards be established outside the AICPA. The APB was replaced by a full-time, seven-member Financial Accounting Standards Board with a broadened membership: only four members may be drawn from among practicing CPAs; the other three represent government, law, financial statement prepares and users, and academe.

But this description does not begin to portray the complex structure of the organization, as we shall see.

The FASB's authoritative pronouncements are labeled *Statements of Financial Accounting Standards* (SFASs). The FASB also issues *Interpretations of Financial Accounting Standards,* which interpret Accounting Research Bulletins and APB Opinions, as well as the FASB's own *Statements.*

As noted in Figure 3-2, the financial accounting standard-setting process involves several entities: the Financial Accounting Foundation (FAF), the board itself, the FASB staff, and the Emerging Issues Task Force.

FIGURE 3-2 Organization of FAF, FASB, and GASB

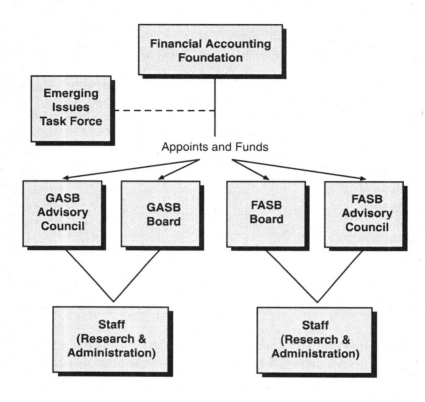

The FAF is the parent organization. Consisting of 15 trustees nominated from organizations with a special knowledge of and interest in financial reporting, it oversees the FASB's budget. These are the nominating organizations:

- American Accounting Association
- American Institute of Certified Public Accountants
- Financial Analysts Federation
- Financial Executives Institute
- Government Finance Officers Association

- Institute of Management Accountants

- National Association of State Auditors, Comptrollers, and Treasurers

- Securities Industry Association

Three other trustees are elected at large, generally from the ranks of banking, law, and government.

In representing a broad spectrum of the financial community, the FASB proper currently consists of two former partners of Big Six CPA firms, two corporate executives, a financial analyst, an academic, and a former practitioner from a small CPA firm. The FASB pursues its investigative activities with a full-time research staff of approximately 50 professionals from various backgrounds. The Financial Accounting Standards Advisory Council (FASAC) advises the FASB on the priorities of its current and proposed projects, on selecting and organizing task forces, and on any other matters the FASB requests.

To help practitioners and their clients implement the provisions of FASB Standards, the FASB's staff periodically issues *Technical Bulletins* to provide timely guidance on implementation issues. These Bulletins allow conformity with FASB pronouncements without the need for the entire FASB Board to issue a new authoritative statement.

While *Technical Bulletins* help clarify conformance to a recently issued FASB authoritative pronouncement, financial statement preparers and users often have questions about issues not "clearly" covered by an existing set of authoritative pronouncements. To fill this void, the Emerging Issues Task Force (EITF) was established in 1984. Chaired by the FASB's Director of Research and Technical Activities, the Task Force is made up of individuals in a position to be aware of issues before they become widespread and before divergent practices regarding them become entrenched. The EITF normally address generally industry-specific issues, rather than those encompassing accounting and financial reporting as a whole. For example, EITF No. 93-5, Accounting for Environmental Liabilities, applies to only those industries with exposure to environmental liabilities. Similarly, EITF No. 93-1, Accounting for Individual Credit Card Acquisitions, only applies to firms that issue credit cards.

If the EITF is unable to reach a consensus on an issue under consideration and it decides that the "problem" merits further action, it will forward the file to the FASB Board for a further deliberation. Conversely, if the Task Force can reach a consensus on an issue, the FASB can usually imply that no Board action is necessary.

Given the importance of FASB standards, the Board seeks always to keep to due process, so much so that it has spent over eleven years deliberating on certain standards. The standard-setting process followed by the Board appears in Figure 3-3. Briefly, the FASB is held to a fixed procedure; before issuing a Statement on Financial Accounting Standards (SFAS), it must take the following steps:

FIGURE 3-3   FASB Standard-Setting Process

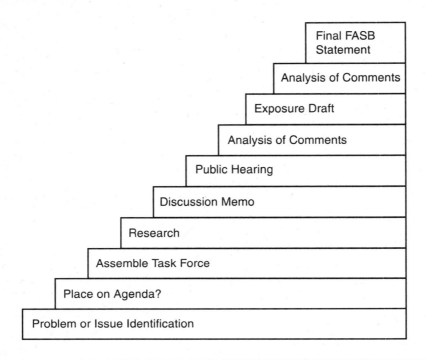

1. Identify the problem or issue and take into account legal or SEC pressures.
2. Decide whether to consider the issue. At this point, the board generally seeks opinion from the FASAC and such professional organizations as Robert Morris Associates, the Institute of Management Accountants (IMA), and the Financial Executives Institute (FEI).
3. Establish a task force to study the problem; usually about 15 people are chosen.
4. Have its research staff investigate the issues.
5. Issue a discussion memo to interested parties. Usually more than 30,000 copies of the discussion memorandum are issued to the public.
6. Hold public hearings and request written comments on the issue. Several hundred responses are usually received.
7. Analyze the results of the investigation, mail responses, and conduct public hearings.
8. If action is appropriate, the Board issues an exposure draft, a preliminary SFAS. The normal exposure period is at least 60 days.

9. Request additional comments on the exposure draft and hold further public hearings.
10. After analyzing the public response, issue a final SFAS.

SFASs are issued in a standard format and reprinted in the *Official Release* section of the *Journal of Accountancy*. Most SFASs contain:

a. A summary.
b. Table of contents.
c. Introduction and other narrative.
d. The actual standard.
e. The FASB members actually voting. (The FAF now requires a 5 to 2 majority to approve new standards.)
f. The basis for a qualifying or dissenting vote of a FASB member.
g. Appendices containing background information, a glossary of terms, numerical and other examples of applying the standard, and other ancillary information.

FASB's Conceptual Framework Project.   In certain situations, an accounting issue may arise for which no precedent has been set and no authoritative pronouncement has been issued. In such cases, the researcher must develop a theoretically justifiable conclusion. A number of organizations and individuals have directed their efforts toward the development of accounting theory in order to provide a framework for resolving issues in a theoretically consistent manner.

The American Accounting Association (AAA), a national professional organization with a membership composed primarily of academicians, sponsors and conducts extensive research of a theoretical or conceptual nature. The AICPA also promotes research in accounting theory and has published a series of *Accounting Research Monographs*. As mentioned previously, the Accounting Principles Board of the AICPA issued four conceptual statements during its existence.

Despite these and other efforts, however, a widely accepted theoretical framework of accounting has not been developed. Recognizing the need for such a framework, the FASB has undertaken a comprehensive, long-range project called the Conceptual Framework Project. This project encompasses a series of pronouncements entitled *Statements of Financial Accounting Concepts* (SFACs), which describe concepts and relationships that underlie financial accounting standards. These pronouncements have addressed or will address such issues as elements of financial statements and their recognition, measurement, and display; capital maintenance; unit of measure; criteria for distinguishing information to be included in financial statements from that which should be provided by other means of financial reporting; and criteria for evaluating and selecting accounting information (qualitative characteristics).

Statements of Financial Accounting Concepts Nos. 1-6.   The first six statements issued under the Conceptual Framework Project are as follows:

1. "Objectives of Financial Reporting of Business Enterprises." This statement sets forth the objectives of general purpose external financial reporting by business enterprises. For example, it states that financial reports should help society better allocate scarce economic resources.
2. "Qualitative Characteristics of Accounting Information." This statement examines the characteristics of accounting information that make the information useful.
3. "Elements of Financial Statements of Business Enterprises." This statement defines ten elements of financial statements of business enterprises: assets, liabilities, equity, investment by owners, distributions to owners, comprehensive income, revenues, expenses, gains, and losses. This SFAC was superseded by SFAC No. 6.
4. "Objectives of Financial Reporting of Nonbusiness Organizations." This statement establishes the objectives of general purpose external financial reporting by nonbusiness organizations.
5. "Recognition and Measurement in Financial Statements." This statement establishes recognition criteria and guidance regarding what information should be incorporated into financial statements. SFAC No. 5 also describes and defines the concept of earnings and what should be included in a full set of an entity's financial statements.
6. "Elements of Financial Statements." (Supersedes SFAC No. 3 and amends portions of SFAC No. 2). This statement redefines the ten interrelated elements of financial statements. It also defines three classes of net assets for not-for-profit organizations as well as accrual accounting and other related concepts.

The purpose of the conceptual framework is to establish objectives and concepts to be used in the development of accounting standards and in the preparation of financial statements, especially where no published standards exist. The project should help produce a constitution for accounting, presenting a coherent set of accounting standards. However, since the FASB did not use full due process in this project, the SFACs are not authoritative; as with APB Statements, CPAs need not justify departures from their guidance.

The bodies discussed so far have been responsible for the accounting pronouncements presented in Appendix A at the end of this chapter. Most of the generally accepted accounting principles are encompassed in this list.

U.S. Securities and Exchange Commission.   The SEC is directed by five Commissioners in Washington, D.C. The Commissioners are assisted by a staff of professionals that includes accountants, lawyers, economists, and securities analysts. These professionals are assigned to the four Divisions in the SEC: Division of Corporation Finance, Division of Market Regulation, Division of Enforcement, and Division of Investment Management. The Commission receives its authoritative status from the public sector rather than the accounting profession. The Securities and Exchange Act of 1934 established the SEC and

charged it with the duty of insuring full and fair disclosures of all material facts relating to publicly traded securities. Power was given to the SEC by Congress to specify the form of documents filed with the Commission and prescribe the accounting principles used in generating the financial data presented in the reports.

The Commission publishes four basic documents delineating its reporting and disclosure requirements:

1. *Regulation S-X*—describes the types of reports that must be filed and the forms that are to be used.
2. *Regulation S-K, Integrated Disclosure Rules*—prescribes the filing requirements for information presented outside the financial statements required under Regulation S-X.
3. *Financial Reporting Releases (FRRs)*—prescribe the accounting principles that must be followed in preparing reports filed with the Commission. These FRRs are analogous to the authoritative pronouncements of the APB or FASB.
4. *Accounting and Auditing Enforcement Releases (AAERs)*—relate to enforcement of the Commission's reporting and disclosure requirements.

The FRRs and AAERs were first issued in 1982. These series of pronouncements replaced the SEC's *Accounting Series Releases* (ASRs), which were issued from 1937 to 1982. Nonenforcement-related ASRs that are still in effect have been codified by the SEC. The Commission has published a topical index to enforcement-related ASRs.

The SEC also publishes a series of *Staff Accounting Bulletins* (SABs), which are unofficial interpretations of the SEC's prescribed accounting principles. These bulletins are analogous to the FASB Technical Bulletins.

The SEC has delegated the major responsibility for accounting standard setting to the FASB but has retained an oversight function. In essence, this is the recognition by the SEC of the authoritative support of accounting principles promulgated by the FASB. The Commission recognizes these principles as acceptable for use in filings with the Commission.

The SEC has broad authority to prescribe accounting principles and informative disclosures to entities in its domain. Such corporations must file an annual Form 10-K report, quarterly Form 10-Q reports, and Form 8-K when significant accounting matters arise (e.g., a change in auditors).

In monitoring the FASB's activities, the SEC has from time to time overruled the FASB or APB, as in the issues of accounting for the investment tax credit, accounting for inflation, and accounting for oil and gas exploration.

In an excellent article from which we quote at length, W. Wade Gaffort and Mary A. Finan summarize the way authoritative pronouncements in federal securities law are spread among federal statutes, SEC rules and regulations, the commission's published view and interpretations, and SEC staff policy.[1]

---

1   Gaffort, W. Wade and Mary A. Finan, "Finding Answers to SEC Questions," pp. 66–70. (Reprinted with permission from *Corporate Accounting*, Summer, 1984, Copyright 1984, Warren, Gorham & Lamont, Inc., 210 South St., Boston, MA 02111. All Rights Reserved.)

Researchers should look to Chapter II of Title 17 of the Code of Federal Regulations (17 CFR) for the official version of SEC rules and regulations. Regulation S-X is the basic accounting regulation, and regulations S-K and 14A have some accounting application. In addition to SEC releases, information services include reference publications, news updates, and books.

> Accountants' involvement with federal securities statutes is generally limited to. . .
>
> • Securities Act of 1933 (1933 Act);
> • Securities Exchange Act of 1934 (1934 Act);
> • Public Utility Holding Company Act of 1935 (PUHCA); and
> • Investment Company Act of 1940 (ICA).

Briefly, the SEC Act of 1933 deals with initial public offerings, while the 1934 Act deals with annual registration statements.

> The PUHCA and the ICA apply [only] to specific types of entities: therefore, accountants encounter those statutes less frequently than the 1933 and 1934 Acts. Those statutes regulate electric and gas public utility holding companies and companies engaged in the business of investing and trading in securities.
>
> **Interpretative case law**. In some areas of federal securities law, notably the general antifraud provisions of the 1934 Act, there are very few formal rules and the law has developed in the traditional "common law" manner, with the courts deciding each case on precedents. In other areas, particularly the registration provisions of the 1933 Act, most of the law is found in the rules, regulations, forms, and policy statements of the Commission.
>
> **SEC rules and regulations**. Federal statutes give the SEC the authority to issue rules and regulations to administer the statutes. Those rules and regulations are formal SEC policy as approved by the five [SEC] commissioners [all other employees of the SEC are staff]. . . . The term "rules and regulations" refers to all rules and regulations adopted by the Commission, including the forms and instructions to the forms that are used for filing of registration statements or periodic reports.
>
> The rules and regulations category serves a variety of purposes; therefore, many different captions are used. Some rules provide definitions of terms in certain statutes or regulations . . . and are called general rules. Other rules are found in regulations, which are a compilation of rules related to a specific subject (e.g., regulation 14A on solicitation of proxies). Still other

rules relate to procedural matters, such as the steps to be followed in proceedings before the Commission, where to file documents, and what type size to use in materials filed with the SEC. . . .

Commission's published views and interpretations. The Codification of Financial Reporting (CFR) Policies is a compendium of the SEC's current published views and interpretations relating to financial reporting. It supplements the rules in regulations S-K and S-X by providing background and rationale for certain of those rules. Prior to its issuance, the Commission's views and interpretations relating to financial reporting were published in Accounting Series Releases (ASRs). ASRs were also used to publish Commission findings on enforcement actions relating to accountants. On April 15, 1982, Financial Reporting Release No. 1 was issued, and it announced that:

- ASRs were being discontinued;
- ASRs were being replaced by two new types of releases—Financial Reporting Releases and Accounting and Auditing Enforcement Releases (AAERs); and
- A codification of relevant existing ASRs that relate to financial accounting matters was being published—its title is Codification of Financial Reporting Policies.

The Commission updates the Codification of Financial Reporting Policies and Regulations S-K and S-X by issuing Financial Reporting Releases. A typical Financial Reporting Release contains the following types of information:

- Background of the topic;
- An evaluation of the comments received on the proposed rules;
- A discussion of the final rules;
- A discussion of transition provisions; and
- The text of new rules.

Generally the Codification of Financial Reporting Policies is updated for only the discussion of final rules. While that information is generally adequate in that it provides the important views of the Commission, accountants occasionally refer to the original release for more detailed background information.

AAERs announce enforcement actions involving accountants. AAERs generally include a summary of the enforcement action, a discussion of the facts, the Commission's conclusions, and any orders issued (e.g., an order to restrict practice before

the SEC by the accountant involved for a specific time period).
Appendix A to AAER No. 1 contains a topical index to
enforcement-related ASRs. It is updated when AAERs are
issued. The index is intended to be only a reference tool.

SEC staff policy. SEC staff policy is followed by the SEC staff
in administering rules, regulations, and statutes. It is not
approved formally by the commissioners; therefore, it cannot be
considered as official rules or interpretations of the Commission. SEC staff policy is published in no-action and interpretative letters, Staff Accounting Bulletins (SABs), correspondence
about accountants' independence, and 1933 and 1934 Act
Industry Guides.

No-action and interpretative letters are published SEC staff
responses to inquiries for interpretations of the application of
statutes or rules and regulations to a particular transaction contemplated by a registrant or to make a general interpretation of
the statutes. The response may indicate the staff will not recommend that the Commission take any action regarding the
proposed transaction or that certain procedures must be followed regarding the transaction.

SABs are interpretations and practices followed by the SEC
staff in the Chief Accountant's Office or the Division of Corporation Finance in administering the disclosure requirements of
the federal securities laws. SABs relate to accounting and
disclosure practices under the rules and regulations. Since the
issuance of SAB No. 40 in January 1981, the SEC has maintained a codification of SABs to make staff accounting bulletins more useful to users. The codification contains 12 topics,
numbered 1 through 12.

In October 1982, the SEC announced in Financial Reporting
Release No. 4 that future correspondence on matters relating
to accountants' independence, which includes staff responses
and letters of inquiry, would be made available for public
inspection and copying. Although this correspondence is quite
specific and situation oriented, the Commission decided to
make it publicly available because several independent
accounting firms expressed an interest in reviewing the correspondence.

The 1933 and 1934 Act Industry Guides are another staff policy
publication of the SEC. Information contained in the Guides
is related to the disclosures made outside the basic financial

statements by companies in certain industries (e.g., oil and gas producing companies and bank holding companies). Of the five current Guides, [the first three] apply to preparation and filing of periodic reports and registration statements under the 1933 and 1934 Acts, and Guide Nos. 4 and 5 apply to preparation and filing of registration statements under the 1933 Act only.

Announcing SEC Policy

The SEC [informs the public of] proposed amendments of rules and regulations, final rules and regulations, the Commission's views and interpretations, and staff policy by using various releases. Proposed amendments of rules and regulations are exposed for a comment period of usually 90 days; however, the comment period can be shortened to 60 or 30 days for matters that are not complex. All releases are identified with "release numbers" that contain a prefix indicating the applicable statute or special type of release and a sequential number that is assigned in the order of issuance by category of prefix.

The prefix and following number are known as the release number. Some common prefixes and their applicable statute or special type of release are shown [below].

Prefix	Applicable Statute or Special Type of Release
33	Securities Act of 1933
34	Securities Exchange Act of 1934
AS	Accounting Series Release
FR	Financial Reporting Release
ER	Accounting and Auditing Enforcement Release

In print, the number would be preceded by the words "Release No." or "Rel. No." Many reference sources exclude the prefix and print the applicable statute, special type of release, or some abbreviation of those. Normally a release contains more than one release number because it applies to more than one statute and possibly is a special type of release. For example, Release Nos. 33-6483, 34-20186 and FR-14 are the same release on an accounting matter that affects filings under the 1933 and 1934 Acts.

Given this vast literature regarding SEC pronouncements, Figure 3-4 summarizes in a hierarchical format the major SEC Authoritative Pronouncements and Publications.[2]

---

2 Miller, Paul B.W. and Jack Robertson, "A Guide to SEC Regulations and Publications: Mastering the Maze," *Research in Accounting Regulation,* 1989, Vol. 3, pp. 239–249.

FIGURE 3-4   A Hierarchy of SEC Authorities and Publications

LEVEL 1:   **Statutes**
i.e., 1933 Securities Act
1934 Securities Exchange Act

LEVEL 2:   **Regulations and Forms**
i.e., Regulation S-X
Regulation S-K

LEVEL 3:   **Commission Releases**

i.e., Financial Reporting Releases
Accounting and Auditing Enforcement Releases
Securities Releases
Exchange Act Releases

LEVEL 4:   **Staff Advice**
i.e., Industry Guides
Staff Accounting Bulletins

Cost Accounting Standards Board.   The Cost Accounting Standards Board (CASB) was established by an Act of Congress in 1971 to increase the uniformity of cost allocations among companies holding large government contracts. Although Congress decided to discontinue the CASB in 1980, it was recreated by Congress in 1989. The newly organized Board has exclusive authority to issue cost accounting standards that govern the measurement, assignment, and allocation of costs on Federal government contracts over $500,000. Of the five CASB members, three are from Federal agencies, one represents industry, and one represents the accounting profession.

To date, the CASB has issued the following standards:

CAS #
401   Consistency in Estimating, Accumulating & Reporting Costs*
402   Consistency in Allocating Costs Incurred for the Same Purpose*
403   Allocation of Home Office Expenses to Segments*
404   Capitalization of Tangible Assets
405   Accounting for Unallowable Costs
406   Cost Accounting Period
407   Use of Standard Cost for Direct Material & Direct Labor
408   Accounting for Costs of Compensated Personal Absence

409 Depreciation of Tangible Capital Assets
410 Allocation of Business Unit General & Administrative Expense to Final Cost Objectives
411 Accounting for Acquisition Costs of Material
412 Composition & Measurement of Pension Costs
413 Adjustment & Allocation of Pension Cost
414 Cost of Money as an Element of the Cost of Facilities Capital
415 Accounting for the Cost of Deferred Compensation
416 Accounting for Insurance Costs
417 Cost of Money as an Element of the Cost of Capital Assets under Construction
418 Allocation of Direct & Indirect Costs
420 Accounting for Independent Research & Development Costs and Bid & Proposal Costs

*Indicates Standard for which an interpretation was issued.
NOTE: CAS 419 was withdrawn.

Internal Revenue Service.   Income tax laws have significantly influenced the development and implementation of GAAP because of the willingness of the accounting profession to accept tax accounting requirements as GAAP. In order not to spend resources keeping two sets of books, many smaller businesses use tax-basis statements as their external financial statements. CPAs must recognize certain reporting problems when the two statements are not identical. The Internal Revenue Service's Interpretations, Private Letter Rulings, Regulations, and other tax accounting pronouncements also affect accounting practice.

Governmental Accounting Standards Board.   Public sector (governmental) accounting is only now reaching the plateau of responsibility and credibility inhabited by private sector (proprietary) accounting, as the Governmental Accounting Standards Board (GASB) develops in a fashion similar to that of the Financial Accounting Standards Board (FASB). Financial reports of local units of government have varied in quality and lacked uniformity for many years because of an absence of clearly defined principles. A body of generally accepted accounting principles (GAAP) for local units of government has evolved slowly. However, given the large value of assets that governmental entities "manage," as well as recent financial crises in municipal units such as New York, Cleveland, and Orange County, California, the financial community has paid increasing attention to governmental units' financial statements.

The first national organization to address government accounting standards was the National Committee on Government Accounting organized by the Municipal Finance Officers Association (MFOA) in 1934. The Committee issued two publications, *Municipal Accounting & Auditing* (1951) and *Classification of Municipal Accounts* (1953).

In 1968, the National Committee on Governmental Accounting published *Government Accounting, Auditing, and Financial Reporting,* known by the acronym GAAFR or simply as "The Blue Book." GAAFR brought together different governmental accounting practices and provided an authoritative source for such accounting; it became the basis for many state laws for uniform municipal accounting (e.g., Michigan Public Act 68-2). During 1973, the MFOA changed the name of the committee to the National Council on Governmental Accounting (NCGA). In 1974, when the AICPA published *Audits of State and Local Governmental Units* (ASLGU), the Audit Guide noted that GAAFR provided a significant source of GAAP for governmental entities.

In 1979, in an attempt to eliminate the accounting differences and to update, clarify, amplify, and reorder the principles of GAAFR, the National Council on Governmental Accounting (NCGA) issued *Statement 1, Governmental Accounting and Financial Reporting Principles.* Statement 1 contained significant modifications to the basic fund accounting and financial reporting philosophy of both GAAFR and the Audit Guide:

1. Eight generic funds were grouped into three categories.
2. Fiduciary funds were to be accounted for as governmental or proprietary funds.
3. Reporting was simplified with five overview financial statements.
4. A Comprehensive Annual Financial Report was developed, organized on a financial reporting pyramid.
5. Reporting a comparison of budget and actual for those funds using budgetary accounts was required.
6. Various levels of acceptable scope of independent audits were redefined.

In addition, financial reporting was improved significantly through standardization of treatment of encumbrances, the use of "all-inclusive" operating statement formats, clarification of reporting of interfund transactions, and elimination of excessively detailed schedules. In 1980, the AICPA issued SOP 80-2, which brought Statement 1 into the Audit Guide by stating financial statements issued in accordance with Statement 1 were in conformity with GAAP. Also in 1980, the Government Finance Officers Association revised the 1968 version of *Governmental Accounting, Auditing, and Financial Reporting.* This work was not intended to establish or authoritatively interpret GAAP for governmental units, but instead provided for an effective application of Statement 1.

Finally, in 1984, after several years of consideration, the Financial Accounting Foundation (FAF) established the GASB (as the successor to the NCGA) to set financial accounting and reporting standards for the public sector (i.e., state and local governmental entities) as the FASB does for all private entities.

The formation of the GASB caused two government organizations [the Government Finance Officers Association (GFOA) and the National Association of State Auditors, Treasurers, and Controllers] to be added to the list of FAF sponsors. The former organization is composed primarily of local operating financial personnel (e.g., municipalities, counties, and port and transit authorities), while the latter consists primarily of state financial officers. Both organizations focus primarily on GASB standards—applicable in the public sector of the economy.

As the successor to the voluntary, part-time National Council on Governmental Accounting, whose standards remain effective until superseded or amended, the GASB received authoritative status for its standards under Rule 203 of the American Institute of Certified Public Accountants' Rules of Conduct and legislation in the various states.

The GASB is a five-member organization, consisting of a former state auditor, a former treasurer of a major city, a university professor, and two retired Big Six accounting firm partners.

The Board's ten-member professional staff works directly with the Board and its task forces, conducts research, participates in public hearings, analyzes oral and written comments received from the public on documents, and prepares drafts of documents for consideration by the Board.

Similar to its FASB counterpart, the GASB has established a practice of due process. Thus, for all major projects, the Board generally will:

- Research the subject to define the issues and to determine the scope of the projects.
- Appoint a task force to advise the Board on the issues and to aid in developing alternative solutions prior to issuance of a discussion document.
- Issue a discussion memorandum or invitation to comment, which will set forth the definition of the problem, scope of the project, and the issues involved; discuss relevant research; and include alternative solutions to the issues identified.
- Hold a public hearing, at which concerned individuals will be encouraged to state their views on the issues contained in the discussion document.
- Issue an exposure draft of a proposed Statement for public comment prior to adoption of a final standard.
- Issue a final Statement. A Statement may be issued by a majority vote of the Board members.

During all of the above steps, the Board will deliberate the issues in meetings open to public observations.

The Board may issue a Statement following exposure for public comment without appointing a task force, issuing a discussion document, or holding a public hearing if, in the judgment of its members, the Board can make an informed decision based on available information.

To date, the GASB has issued 27 authoritative Statements:

Number
1   "Authoritative Status of NCGA Pronouncements and AICPA Industry Guide." (1985)

2   "Financial Reporting of Deferred Compensation Plans Adopted Under Provisions of Internal Revenue Code Section 457." (1986)

3   "Deposits with Financial Institutions, Investments (including Repurchase Agreements), and Reverse Repurchase Agreements." (1986)

4   "Applicability of FASB Statement No. 87, 'Employers' Accounting for Pensions,' to State and Local Governmental Employers." (1986)

5   "Disclosure of Pension Information by Public Employee Retirement Systems and State and Local Governmental Employers." (1986)

6   "Accounting and Financial Reporting for Special Assessments." (1987)

7   "Advance Refundings Resulting in Defeasance of Debt." (1987)

8   "Applicability of FASB Statement No. 93, 'Recognition of Depreciation by Not-for-Profit Organizations,' to Certain State and Local Governmental Entities." (1988)

9   "Reporting Cash Flows of Proprietary and Nonexpensible Trust Funds and Government Entities that Use Proprietary Fund Accounting." (1989)

10 "Accounting and Financial Reporting for Risk Financing and Related Insurance Issues." (1989)

11 "Measurement Focus and Basis of Accounting—Governmental Fund Operating Statements." (1990)

12 "Disclosure of Information on Post-Employment Benefits Other Than Pension Benefits by State and Local Government Employers." (1990)

13 "Accounting for Operating Leases with Scheduled Rent Increases." (1990)

14 "The Financial Reporting Entity." (1991)

15 "Governmental College and University Accounting and Financial Reporting Models." (1991)

16 "Accounting for Compensated Absences." (1993)

17 "Measurement Focus and Basis of Accounting—Governmental Fund Operating Statements: Amendment of the Effective Dates of GASB Statement No. 11 and Related Statements." (1993)

18 "Accounting for Municipal Solid Waste Landfill Closure and Post-Closure Care Costs." (1994)

19 "Governmental College and University Omnibus Statement: An Amendment of GASB Statements Nos. 10 and 15." (1994)

20 "Accounting and Financial Reporting for Proprietary Funds and Other Governmental Entities that Use Proprietary Fund Accounting." (1994)

21 "Accounting for Escheat Property." (1994)

22 "Accounting for Taxpayer-Assessed Tax Revenues in Governmental Funds." (1994)

23 "Accounting and Financial Reporting for Refundings of Debt Reported by Proprietary Activities." (1994)

24 "Accounting and Financial Reporting for Certain Grants and Other Financial Assistance." (1994)

25 "Financial Reporting for Defined Benefit Pension Plans and Note Disclosures for Defined Contribution Plans." (1995)

26   "Financial Reporting for Postemployment Healthcare Plans Administered
     by Defined Benefit Pension Plans." (1995)
27   "Accounting for Pensions by State and Local Governmental Employers."
     (1995)

   Similar to its FASB counterpart, the GASB has an advisory council. The
Governmental Accounting Standards Advisory Council (GASAC) is responsible
for consulting with the GASB as to major policy questions, technical issues on
the Board's agenda, project priorities, matters likely to require the attention of the
GASB, selection and organization of task forces, and such other matters as may
be requested by the GASB or its chairperson. The GASAC also is responsible for
helping to develop the GASB's annual budget and aiding the Financial Accounting Foundation in raising funds for the Board. At present, the Council has 22
members who are broadly representative of preparers, attestors, and users of financial information.

Professional Organizations.   Many professional organizations that do not
set accounting standards nevertheless influence directly or indirectly the setting
of those standards.

- The Institute of Management Accountants (IMA), through its Management
  Accounting Practices Committee, provides formal input to the FASB, although
  it does not establish standards.
- The National Association of State Auditors, Controllers, and Treasurers is
  an information clearinghouse and research base for state financial officials.
  Although it publishes no journal, the Association performs financial management projects for state fiscal officers, and it appoints members to the
  Financial Accounting Foundation.
- The Financial Executives Institute (FEI) influences accounting standards development through its Panel on Accounting Principles, which makes recommendations on discussion memoranda issued by the FASB. The FEI also conducts its
  own research through the Financial Executives Research Foundation.
- The Securities Industry Associates (SIA), which represents investment bankers and manages the portfolios of large institutional investors, and the Financial Analysts Federation are typical of the kind of organizations that influence
  the setting of standards and the shaping of GAAP because they help to select
  members of the Financial Accounting Foundation, which in turn selects the
  members of the FASB and the GASB. Since these groups represent users of
  financial statements, they usually favor standards providing for additional disclosures, just as the IMA, representing preparers, protects the interests of its
  members.
- The academic arm of accounting, the American Accounting Association (AAA),
  emphasizes the need for a theoretical foundation for accounting and influences standard setting through the research and analysis of accounting

concepts presented in committee reports and in its quarterly journal, *The Accounting Review.*

Figure 3-5 summarizes the constituencies and the missions of organizations affecting standard setting and the shaping of GAAP.

Generally Accepted Accounting Principles

According to APB Statement No.4, GAAP is "a technical accounting term which encompasses the conventions, rules, and procedures necessary to define accepted accounting practice at a particular time." This wide but wary definition implies two truths:

1. GAAP is not a static, well-defined set of accounting principles, but a fluid set of principles based on current accounting thought and practice. GAAP changes in response to change in the business environment.
2. GAAP is not composed of mutually exclusive accounting principles. Alternative principles for similar transactions may be considered equally acceptable. The researcher does not quit, then, when one acceptable principle is found.

GAAP performs two major functions:

1. *Measurement.* GAAP requires that revenues of a given period should be recognized (i.e., matched) with all expenses that were incurred to generate those revenues (e.g., depreciating fixed assets and recognizing stock options and pension liabilities). Besides attempting to measure periodic income objectively, the measurement principle focuses on valuation of financial statements accounts (e.g., reporting inventories at the lower of cost or market valuations).
2. *Disclosure.* GAAP provides information necessary for the users' decision models (e.g., methods to group accounts and descriptive terminology, as in reporting lease obligations in the footnotes). However, GAAP does not require disclosure of certain macroeconomic factors (e.g., interest and unemployment rates) often of interest to the entity, bankers, and other financial statement users.

CPAs may not express an opinion that the financial statements are presented in conformity with GAAP if the statements depart materially from an accounting principle promulgated by an "authoritative body" (i.e., a senior technical committee) designated by the AICPA Council, such as the APB and the FASB.

While opinions from these bodies provide the "substantial authoritative support" necessary to create GAAP, other sources of GAAP are available. Most notable are standard industry practices that provide material for GAAP either when a practice addresses a principle that does not exist in GAAP or when a

FIGURE 3-5 The Role of Professional Accounting Organizations in Developing GAAP

Organization	Principal Membership	Principal Mission	Professional Journal
*1. American Accounting Association (AAA)	Accounting academicians	Helps develop a logical, theoretical basis for accounting. Promotes research and education in accounting.	The Accounting Review
*2. American Institute of Certified Public Accountants (AICPA)	Certified Public Accountants	Its various committees have issued authoritative pronouncements on accounting principles and auditing standards. Conducts programs of research, continuing education, surveillance of practice, jurisdiction consistency, and communications.	Journal of Accountancy
*3. Association of Government Accountants (AGA)	Federal, state, and local government accountants	Professional society of accountants, auditors, comptrollers, and budget officers employed by federal, state, and local governments in management and administrative positions. Monitors the activities of and often provides input to the Government Accounting Standards Board (GASB).	Government Accountants' Journal
*4. Financial Analysts Federation	Financial analysts and Chartered Financial Analysts	Promotes the development of improved standards of investment research and portfolio management. An organization of primary users of accounting information, it represents those who analyze information and provide professional advice on investment matters.	Financial Analysts Journal
*5. Financial Executives Institute (FEI)	Corporate financial executives	Professional organization of financial and management executives performing duties of a controller, treasurer, or VP-finance, primarily from large corporations. Sponsors research activities through its affiliated Financial Executives Research Foundation.	FE: The Magazine for Financial Executives
*6. Governmental Finance Officers Association (GFOA)	State and local public finance officials	Provides technical service center and technical inquiry service for public finance officials. Monitors the activities of and often provides input to the GASB.	Governmental Finance Review

FIGURE 3-5 (continued)

*7. Institute of Internal Auditors (IIA)	Internal auditors and Certified Internal Auditors	Cultivates, promotes, and disseminates knowledge concerning internal auditors. Sponsors research on the internal auditor's role in promoting more reliable financial information.	*The Internal Auditor*
*8. Institute of Management Accountants (IMA)	Corporate controllers and financial officers and Certified Management Accountants	Conducts research primarily on management accounting methods and procedures, and has recently increased its role in the development of financial accounting standards.	*Management Accounting*
*9. National Association of State Auditors, Controllers, and Treasurers	State financial officials	Serves as an information clearinghouse and research base for state financial officials.	
10. Robert Morris Associates	Bank officers	Promotes studies on comparative industry practices to provide benchmarks against which to judge corporate performance.	*Journal of Commercial Bank Lending*
11. Securities Industry Association (SIA)	Broker dealers in securities	Monitors and provides input to stockbrokers regarding SEC, stock exchanges (e.g., NYSE and AMEX), and congressional actions.	*Securities Industry Trends*

* Also appoints members to the Financial Accounting Foundation.

practice seems to conflict with GAAP. In either case, management must state the case for the practice, and the CPA must evaluate the case to ascertain whether the practice violates established GAAP. In addition, if "unusual circumstances" would make following the normal procedure misleading, management must disclose departures from authoritative guidelines and justify the alternative principle.

The FASB arrives at GAAP by relating principles to three objectives of financial reporting set out in Statement of Financial Accounting Concepts No. 1. Financial reporting should provide information that:

1. Is useful to present and potential investors and creditors and other users in making rational investment, credit, and similar decisions. The information should be comprehensible to those who have a reasonable understanding of business and economic activities and are willing to study the information with reasonable diligence.

2. Helps present and potential investors and creditors and other users in assessing the amounts, timing, and uncertainty of prospective cash receipts from dividends or interest and the proceeds from the sale, redemption, or maturity of securities or loans. Since investors' and creditors' cash flows are related to enterprise cash flows, financial reporting should provide information to help investors, creditors, and others assess the amounts, timing, and uncertainty of prospective net cash inflows to the related enterprise.
3. Clarifies the economic resources of an enterprise, the claims to those resources (obligations of the enterprise to transfer resources to other entities and owners' equity), and the effects of transactions, events, and circumstances that change its resources and claims to those resources.

To minimize the haphazard establishment of GAAP, standards emerge according to these objectives, which, in turn, provide standards necessary for measuring the effectiveness of existing and proposed conventions, rules, and procedures that define accepted accounting practice.

Authoritative Support.   Unlike the natural scientist, the accounting practitioner does not search for natural laws but rather attempts to discover a consensus among users of financial information. Since the accounting process is an artificially created mathematical model of an entity, the accountant relies heavily on authoritative support in determining the principles and procedures used to implement the accounting model.

As we said earlier, CPAs may not attest to the validity of financial statements (i.e., may not express an opinion that the statements are presented in conformity with GAAP) if the statement departs materially from an accounting principle promulgated by an authoritative body (i.e., a senior technical committee) designated by the AICPA Council, such as the APB, the FASB, and the GASB. However, a CPA may justify an alternative principle if unusual circumstances would make following the normal principles misleading. That is, under Rule 203 of the AICPA's Code of Professional Conduct, if the entity's management feels the circumstances do not warrant compliance with the standard, an exception can be taken. Under these circumstances, the auditor's report must clearly disclose the nature of and the reason for the exception in the financial statements.

The Hierarchy of GAAP.[3]   Accountants in general agree that a body of generally accepted accounting principles exists. The components of GAAP that currently exist can be depicted in a hierarchy. This hierarchy shows the researcher where to begin in a search for a solution to the problem or issue under review. Figures 3-6 and 3-7 present the basic components of the hierarchy for Financial Statement GAAP and Government GAAP, respectively, as five different levels. Those in level one have the highest level of authority.

---

3   Statement on Auditing Standards No. 69, *The Meaning of Present Fairly in Conformity with Generally Accepted Accounting Principles in the Independent Auditor's Report*, AICPA, 1991.

FIGURE 3-6   Basic Principles and Assumptions Underlying Financial
Reporting

LEVEL   **COMPONENTS**

1   Pronouncements of an Authoritative Body designated by the AICPA
           Council in Rule 203 of the Code of Professional Conduct.

           a. FASB Statements and Interpretations
           b. APB Opinions
           c. AICPA Accounting Research Bulletins
           d. Rules and Interpretative Releases of the SEC for SEC regis-
               trants

2   Pronouncements of bodies composed of expert accountants who
           follow a due process procedure; such pronouncements have been
           cleared by a body referred to in level 1.

           a. Cleared AICPA Industry Audit and Accounting Guides
           b. Cleared AICPA Statements of Position (SOPs)
           c. FASB Technical Bulletins

3   Pronouncements of bodies organized by the AICPA or FASB but
           that do not necessarily go through due process procedures.

           a. AcSEC Practice Bulletins having been cleared by the FASB
           b. Consensus Positions of the FASB Emerging Issues Task Force

4   Practices or pronouncements that are widely recognized as being
           generally accepted because they represent prevalent practice in a
           particular industry, or the knowledgeable application to specific cir-
           cumstances of pronouncements that are generally accepted.

           a. AICPA Accounting Interpretations
           b. Implementation Guides by the FASB Staff (Questions and
               Answers series)
           c. Notable Industry Practices
           d. Uncleared SOPs, and audit and accounting guides

5   Other Accounting Literature

           a. APB Statements
           b. AICPA Issues Papers
           c. FASB Concepts Statements
           d. International Accounting Standards Committee Statements
           e. AICPA Technical Practice Aids
           f. Textbooks
           g. Journal articles and monographs

FIGURE 3-7   Basic Principles and Assumptions Underlying Government Reporting

LEVEL	COMPONENTS
1	Pronouncements of an Authoritative Body

    a. GASB Pronouncements (Statements and Interpretations)
    b. NCGA Pronouncements acknowledged by the GASB
    c. FASB and AICPA Pronouncements
    NOTE: If the accounting treatment of a transaction or event is not specified by a pronouncement of either 1a or 1b, then 1c is presumed to apply.

2   Pronouncements of bodies composed of expert accountants who follow a due process procedure.

    a. GASB Technical Bulletins
    b. Cleared AICPA Industry Audit and Accounting Guides, such as:
         Audits of State and Local Governmental Units
         Audits of Certain Nonprofit Organizations
         Audits of Colleges and Universities
    c. Cleared AICPA Statements of Position

3   Consensus positions of the GASB, EITF, and cleared AcSEC practice bulletins for state and local government.

4   Practices or pronouncements that are widely recognized as being generally accepted because they represent prevalent practice in a particular industry, or the knowledgeable application to specific circumstances of pronouncements that are generally accepted.

    a. Uncleared SOPs and Audit and Accounting Guides
    b. Questions and Answers issued by GASB staff
    c. Industry practice

5   Other Accounting Literature

    a. GASB Statements of Financial Accounting Concepts
    b. Elements of the Financial Statement Hierarchy
    c. Textbooks
    d. Journal articles

The foundation for this hierarchy contains the basic assumption or concepts of financial or government accounting. This foundation includes basic assumptions and principles underlying financial reporting: e.g., the going-concern assumption, substance over form, neutrality, the accrual basis, conservatism, materiality, objectivity, consistency, and full disclosure.

Levels one through four contain the components of four groups of reference sources containing established accounting principles. Level five provides other accounting literature in the absence of an established authoritative accounting principle as authorized by Rule 203 of the Code of Professional Conduct.

The following additional information about the levels of Financial Statement GAAP should enhance the reader's understanding of the items within each level.

Level 1. Pronouncements of an authoritative body designated by the AICPA, that officially establish GAAP, including:

    a. FASB Statements of Financial Accounting Standards (SFASs) and Interpretations.

    b. Thirty-one Opinions of the AICPA's Accounting Principles Board (APBOs).

    c. Fifty-one Accounting Research Bulletins (ARBs), which were issued by the Committee on Accounting Procedure (CAP) of the AICPA.

    d. Rules And Interpretative Releases issued by the Securities and Exchange Commission. Since the SEC has the ultimate authority to establish GAAP for publicly listed entities, these pronouncements have the highest level of authority that applies specifically to SEC registrants.

In short, FASB statements supersede some APB opinions, which supersede some ARB statements, but those unsuperseded APB opinions and ARB statements are still effective. More recently issued standards supersede earlier ones. A FASB interpretation clarifies, explains, or elaborates on prior FASB, APB, and ARB statements, and has the same authority they do.

Level 2. Pronouncements of bodies of expert accountants who follow a "due process" of deliberating and issuing accounting statements.

    a. AICPA Industry Audit Guides and Accounting Guides, which normally are reviewed by the Institute's Accounting Standards Executive Committee (AcSEC) and cleared by the FASB.

    b. AICPA Statements of Position (SOPs), which have been reviewed by AcSEC and cleared by the FASB.

    c. FASB Technical Bulletins, which provide guidance in applying authoritative pronouncements.

Level 3. This level includes AcSEC Practice Bulletins that have been cleared by the FASB, and also includes consensus positions of the FASB Emerging Issues Task Force (EITF).

Level 4. Included in this level are the AICPA Interpretations as well as implementation guides (referred to as "Questions and Answers") issued by the FASB staff. Also included in this level are the uncleared AICPA Statements of Position and uncleared audit and accounting guides (cleared SOPs and guides appear in level 3) and practices widely recognized in a particular industry.

Level 5. This level provides other accounting literature that the researcher could reference in the absence of a higher-level authority.

While reference to an authoritative pronouncement usually provides adequate support for an accounting decision, often accountants forced to rely on lower levels of support must build a case involving multiple references. Figure 3-8 provides a division between primary, self-supporting references and secondary, non-self-supporting references.

In researching an issue, often this question arises: Where does one start and when can one stop the research process? To begin the research, one would focus on the primary authoritative support, which has the highest level of authority according to the hierarchy of GAAP. If no primary sources are cited, then one would drop down and review the secondary support.

If the researcher determines that the answer to the question is located in a primary authoritative support, the research process can stop since these sources are sufficient for a conclusion. However, if the source cited is secondary support, additional research is needed since any secondary source individually is insufficient authority. The researcher must keep in mind that many research questions will not be clear-cut and, therefore, professional judgment is a key element in deciding when to stop the research process.

Economic Consequences.

Selecting among possible accounting alternatives often affects economic decisions. For example, companies adopting the provisions of FASB Statement No. 96 could "transfer" part of their Deferred Tax Liability from a liability on the balance sheet to revenue on the income statement, as income tax rates fall; the reverse would occur as income tax rates rise. However, the provisions of APB Opinion No. 11 would not affect current income calculations as the tax rates fluctuate. Thus, the researcher must recognize macroeconomic factors in planning and selecting accounting principles.

Rappaport[4] further found that the promulgation of financial accounting standards can affect economic behavior and wealth distribution in three ways. The standards can influence intended external users (e.g., competitors and stockholders), unintended external users (e.g., competitors, labor unions, and special interest groups) and internal users (e.g., corporate management). For example, assume that the research suggests that a significant piece of equipment should be expensed immediately rather than continue to be capitalized over several years, since its future value "seemed" impaired. This reduction in income could

---

4   Rappaport, Alfred, "Economic Impact of Accounting Standards—Implications for the FASB," *The Journal of Accountancy* Vol. 2 (May 1977); pp. 89–97.

FIGURE 3-8   Accounting Authoritative Support

Primary Authoritative Support

Sources that provide sufficient authoritative support for including a particular accounting principle within GAAP.

A. General Application to the Field of Accounting
    1. FASB and GASB Statements of Financial and Governmental Accounting Standards
    2. FASB and GASB Interpretations
    3. Opinions of the Accounting Principles Board
    4. Accounting Research Bulletins of the Committee on Accounting Procedures
    5. Consensus Positions of EITF

B. Special Application to Certain Entities
    1. AICPA Industry Accounting Guides
    2. AICPA Statements of Position
    3. Regulations of the Securities and Exchange Commission
    4. Statements of the Cost Accounting Standards Board
    5. Interpretations of the Cost Accounting Standards Board

Secondary Authoritative Support

Sources that support inclusion of particular accounting principles within GAAP, but individually are not sufficient authoritative support.

A. Official Publications of Authoritative Bodies
    1. FASB Statements of Financial Accounting Concepts
    2. GASB Concept Statements
    3. FASB Technical Bulletins
    4. APB Statements
    5. Interpretations of APB Opinions

B. Other Sources of Information
    1. Substantive industrial practices
    2. Pronouncements of industry regulatory authorities
    3. Published research studies of authoritative professional and industrial societies
    4. Publications of recognized industry associations
    5. Accounting research monographs of the AICPA
    6. SEC Staff Accounting Bulletins
    7. Pronouncements of the IFAC and other international accounting bodies
    8. Accounting textbooks and reference books authored by recognized authorities in the field

adversely impact the company's earnings per share and, thus, stock price; it could reduce the union member's profit sharing payouts or make their competitors' financial statements look relatively stronger, enabling them to attract new investors; and it could reduce the bonuses available to corporate management, thereby causing them to relocate to their competitors' organizations. The above examples demonstrate that the "Law of Unintended Consequences" often generates many unexpected ramifications from the researcher's decisions. Nonetheless, the researcher is ethically bound to follow GAAP to help report accurate financial information—regardless of future economic consequences.

International Accounting

The present condition of international accounting is characterized largely by a collection of authoritative pronouncements of each individual country. This makes the task of comparing companies across national boundaries cumbersome and potentially confusing.

Efforts have increased in recent years to move toward international standards. The movement toward harmonization has included the work of individual scholars as well as the activities of supranational groups. Included in the latter category are the International Federation of Accountants (IFAC), the International Accounting Standards Committee (IASC), the Organization for Economic Cooperation and Development (OECD), and the European Economic Community (EEC).

The IASC has moved to the forefront as an international accounting standards-setting body. R.S. Olusegun Wallace attributes the IASC's success to the following:[5]

1. The increasing internationalization of business and finance, which makes global harmonization of accounting and disclosure practices desirable.
2. The composite nature of its standards and its preoccupation with topics of a general nature.
3. Its evolutionary strategy.
4. The absence of a rival organization with keen and prolonged interest in the development and marketing of global accounting standards.

The International Organization of Securities Commissions (IOSCO) is assisted by the IASC when providing acceptable International Accounting Standards that are acceptable for multinational securities and other international offerings.

Much progress to worldwide standards is underway. For example, Harding's[6] 1993 study of the IASC's membership found that the vast majority of countries possess reporting requirements that adhere to IAS standards. He also concluded

---

5 Wallace, R. S. Olusegun, "Survival Strategies of a Global Organization: The Case of the International Accounting Standards Committee," *Accounting Horizons,* Vol. 4 (June 1990); pp. 1–22.

6 Harding, Terry, "Towards International Harmonization," *Accountancy,* December 1993, Vol. 12, Issue 1204, p. 94.

that more than a third of the respondents worldwide refer explicitly to compliance with IAS standards in their annual reports.

Recently, Arthur Wyatt (former member of the FASB and former Chair of the International Accounting Standards Committee) and Joseph Yospe (Officer, AT&T Capital Corporation) urged that, in light of the worldwide competition for capital, all financial information be prepared in accordance with International Accounting Standards. This harmonization can help in comparing financial statements from differing countries. However, despite many international companies seeking to trade their securities in U.S. markets, this worldwide view has not yet been adopted. Nonetheless, this harmonization should be here relatively soon—as is emerging presently in Europe under the European Union's 4th Directive.[7] Furthermore, the International Accounting Standards Committee recently approved ten revised international accounting standards (IAS) to complete its comparability and improvements project. This set of standards includes such "main-line" topics as Accounting for Inventories, Research and Development Costs, and Retirement Benefit Costs, thereby indicating that such harmonization should be eventually approved in the United States.

Nonetheless, compliance remains voluntary, and the achievement of international standards remains far from reality. For example, even though the IASC has issued 31 standards since its inception in 1973, as well as a Framework for the Preparation and Presentation of Financial Statements, adherence to these pronouncements is purely voluntary and no provision yet exists for enforcement of the requirements. Thus, diversity rather than harmony characterizes international accounting today.

For example, Donald E. Wygal, David E. Stout, and James Volpi contrasted how a series of identical transactions would be reported on U.S., United Kingdom, German, and Australian financial statements.[8] Primarily due to differences in the accounting for extraordinary items, deferred income taxes, and prior period adjustments, the final results varied radically.

Thus, according to Richard D. Fitzgerald:[9]

> Accounting principles and reporting practices are forms of communication which, in theory, should move across national boundaries as freely as the business practices they are intended to reflect. In truth, however, these procedures mirror the disparate economic and social environments of their respective nations and regions.

---

7   Gould, John D., "A Second Opinion on International Accounting Standards," *The CPA Journal,* January 1995, pp. 50–52.

8   Wygal, Donald E., David E. Stout, and James Volpi, "Reporting Practices in Four Countries," *Management Accounting*, (December, 1987); pp. 37–42.

9   Fitzgerald, Richard D., "International Accounting and Reporting: Where in the World Are We Headed?" *Price Waterhouse Review,* (Spring 1983); p. 16. Reprinted with permission of Price Waterhouse.

> Accounting is the language of business. And, as with all languages, unless the grammar and meanings are reasonably clear, the message may be misunderstood. Differences in languages, laws, and conventions from one nation to the next complicate useful communication. So it is with accounting.
>
> The generally accepted accounting principles familiar to accountants in the United States may not be those used by their foreign counterparts in the preparation of financial statements. To the American businessman the contrast often is startling.

In order to harmonize these divergent worldwide principles, the IASC asked its member bodies to see that:

> published financial statements comply with these standards, or that there is disclosure of the extent to which they do not [comply], and [to] persuade governments, authorities controlling securities markets, and the industrial and business community that published financial statements should comply with these standards.[10]

For example, the General Electric Company, in the Statement of Financial Responsibility section of its 1993 annual report, mentions the use of accounting principles that are consistent with standards issued by the International Accounting Standards Committee. This is an excellent example of an international company disclosing its accounting principles. More U.S. companies should follow in its footsteps.

Gary W. Meek[11] details six levels of harmony among accounting standards.

1. *No Accommodation to Foreign Readers.* Financial statements are prepared according to local accounting principles that retain the native language and currency. This approach assumes a general applicability and usefulness in other countries, and leaves it to the reader to interpret the report. This is the prevalent practice of companies domiciled in the United States and in France.
2. *Convenience Translations.* Financial statements are still prepared using local accounting principles, but the text portions are translated into another language. Monetary units are not translated. In a sense, this approach assumes that to "read" something familiar is better than nothing at all, but it still does little to accommodate the foreign reader. German and Swiss companies often adopt this approach.

---

10 Ibid, p. 18

11 Meek, Gary W., "Competition Spurs Worldwide Harmonization," *Management Accounting,* (August 1986); pp. 47–49. Reprinted with permission of the National Association of Accountants.

3. *Convenience Statements*. These are convenience translations taken one step further. Here, the monetary amounts are translated as well (usually by applying the year-end foreign exchange rate to all amounts in the financial statements), so that both the text and monetary amounts are familiar to the audience-of-interest. Convenience statements are issued by some European and some Japanese companies.

4. *Disclosure of Impacts of Differences in Accounting Principles*. For the particular audience-of-interest, the financial statements include a special footnote or supplementary schedule reconciling net income (and sometimes asset and liability accounts) on the basis of the generally accepted accounting principles of the home country to a net income amount based on the accounting principles of the country of the audience-of-interest. This is the minimum requirement for reporting to the U.S. Securities & Exchange Commission by non-U.S. companies in their 20-F reports. Also, the Dutch Phillips Company routinely includes this disclosure in its annual report to U.S. shareholders.

5. *Multiple Reporting*. "Primary" financial statements are prepared for local audiences in the native language and using local accounting principles. "Secondary" financial statements also are prepared for audiences in other countries, the characteristics of which include:

   • The text material is in the language of the "other country."
   • The generally accepted accounting principles and disclosure criteria used are those of the "other country."
   • The monetary amounts are expressed in the currency of the "other country" (as in convenience statements).
   • Essentially, this approach requires a company to keep more than one set of books. It is typical for today's large Japanese multinationals.

6. *World Standards*. Here the company attempts to transcend national reporting differences by synthesizing the practices around the world. The financial statements, however, may or may not be consistent with the recommendations of the International Accounting Standards Committee. Each company selects what in its own management's opinion represents the best of the practices in the world. Sometimes these financial statements will be appended to the local set, but they may actually be the primary financial statements. The statements of the Swiss CIBA-GEIGY Ltd. illustrate the former, while those of the Dutch/U.K. Royal Dutch/Shell illustrate the latter.

Summary

    This chapter has presented an overview of the bodies that set standards in accounting, the process of standard setting, the types of authoritative pronouncements, the meaning of GAAP, the hierarchy of GAAP, and the current status of international accounting. Because GAAP is not a static, well-defined set of accounting principles, but, rather, is a fluid set of principles based on current accounting thought and practice, the researcher needs to be aware of changes in pronouncements. And, because GAAP is not composed of mutually exclusive accounting principles, research in accounting does not consist of searching for a single acceptable principle, but for alternative principles that must be judged in the light of their place in a hierarchy.

Discussion Questions

1. Discuss the environmental factors that influence the standard-setting process.

2. Identify the authoritative accounting pronouncements of the AICPA, FASB, and GASB.

3. What appears to be an underlying reason for the establishment of accounting standards?

4. Describe the rule-making or due-process procedures of the FASB in the establishment of a standard.

5. What is the FASB's Conceptual Framework Project? Of what benefit is this Project to the practitioner?

6. Identify the authoritative publications of the SEC, CASB, and AICPA.

7. What constitutes generally accepted accounting principles?

8. What is the purpose for the establishment of the hierarchy of GAAP?

9. What is meant by the term *authoritative support*?

10. What are the implications of GAAP and authoritative support to the researcher?

11. To conduct efficient research, where should one start in reviewing the accounting or auditing literature in search of a solution to a problem?

12. Compare the FASB's Statements in the hierarchy of Financial Statement GAAP and Government GAAP.

13. How can the promulgation of an accounting standard impact economic behavior? Can you discuss a specific example?

14. Distinguish between primary authoritative support and secondary authoritative support.

15. What two governmental organizations were added to the list of sponsoring organizations of the Financial Accounting Foundation (FAF) due to the establishment of the GASB's authoritative status?

16. What standards did the IASC develop?

17. Why are accountants generally more concerned with Regulation S-X and, to a lesser extent, Regulation S-K and 14A than with most other regulations?

18. What information is usually contained in a Financial Reporting Release?

Appendix A
Accounting Pronouncements

Committee on Accounting Procedures: 1938–1959

Accounting Research Bulletins (ARBs)

Number		Year Issued
43	Restatement and Revision of Accounting Research Bulletins Nos. 1–42	1953
44	Declining-Balance Depreciation 1954, revised	1958
45	Long-Term Construction-Type Contracts	1955
46	Discontinuance of Dating Earned Surplus	1956
47	Accounting for Costs of Pension Plans	1956
48	Business Combinations	1957
49	Earnings per Share	1958
50	Contingencies	1958
51	Consolidated Financial Statements	1959

Accounting Principles Board (APB): 1959–1973

APB Opinions

Number		Year Issued
1	New Depreciation Guidelines and Rules	1962
2	Accounting for the "Investment Credit"	1962
3	The Statement of Source and Application of Funds	1963
4	Accounting for the "Investment Credit" (Amending No. 2)	1964
5	Reporting of Leases in Financial Statement of Lessee	1964
6	Status of Accounting Research Bulletins	1965
7	Accounting for Leases in Financial Statements of Lessors	1966
8	Accounting for the Cost of Pension Plans	1966
9	Reporting the Results of Operations	1966
10	Omnibus Opinion—1966	1966
11	Accounting for Income Taxes	1967
12	Omnibus Opinion—1967	1967
13	Amending Paragraph 6 of *APB Opinion No. 9,* Application to Commercial Banks	1969
14	Accounting for Convertible Debt and Debt Issued with Stock Purchase Warrants	1969
15	Earnings per Share	1969
16	Business Combinations	1970
17	Intangible Assets	1970

APB Statements

Financial Accounting Standards Board (FASB): 1973 to present

Statements of Financial Accounting Standards (SFASs)

ATTESTATION STANDARDS-SETTING ENVIRONMENT AND PROFESSIONAL JUDGMENT

Learning Objectives

After completing this chapter, you should understand:

- Attest services and standards.
- The environment of the attest standard-setting process.
- Authoritative auditing support.
- The role of auditing in the public sector.
- The hierarchy of the Code of Professional Conduct.
- The role of professional judgment in the research process.
- The international dimensions of auditing.

Attestation services are increasingly being demanded of the accounting profession by society. In the past, attest services were normally limited to expressing an audit opinion on historical financial statements based upon an audit that followed Generally Accepted Auditing Standards (GAAS). However, in more recent times, professional accountants have been requested to render opinions on representations that are other than historical financial statements. The concern of the practitioner, therefore, was that there did not exist standards or guidelines to meet the demands of society. As a result, the AICPA developed attest standards and related interpretations to provide a general framework for attest engagements.[1]

The term "attest" has the meaning of providing assurance to the reliability of information. The AICPA has defined an attest engagement as follows:

> An attest engagement is one in which a practitioner is engaged to issue or does issue a written communication that expresses a conclusion about the reliability of a written assertion that is the responsibility of another party.[2]

Whether the attest service is for the traditional financial statements audit or the relatively new services of reporting on an entity's internal control structure or prospective financial information, the professional accountant must follow certain guidelines and standards in rendering these services. In conducting an attest engagement, the professional accountant reviews and makes tests of the accounting records deemed necessary to obtain sufficient evidence to render an opinion. Choosing the accounting records and other information to review and deciding upon the extent to which they should be examined are strictly matters of professional judgment, as many authoritative pronouncements emphasize.

Figure 4-1 presents the major elements of the attest environment that face the accountant in conducting attest research with Figure 4-2 presenting an overview of attest engagements and guidelines the researcher should be familiar with in conducting research. This chapter will focus on an overview of this attest standard-setting environment, the auditing standard-setting process, authoritative auditing pronouncements, and the role of professional judgment in the research process. The chapter also includes a summary of the attestation standards, compilation and review standards, as well as an overview of auditing in the public sector and the international dimensions of auditing.

Attestation Services and Standards

Recently, as the range of attest services has expanded, many CPAs have found it more difficult to apply the basic concepts underlying Generally Accepted

---

1   AICPA *Professional Standards,* Vol. 1 (Chicago: Commerce Clearing House), AT Section—Introduction.

2   AICPA *Professional Standards,* Vol. 1 (Chicago: Commerce Clearing House), AT Section 100.01.

FIGURE 4-1 Attest Research Environment

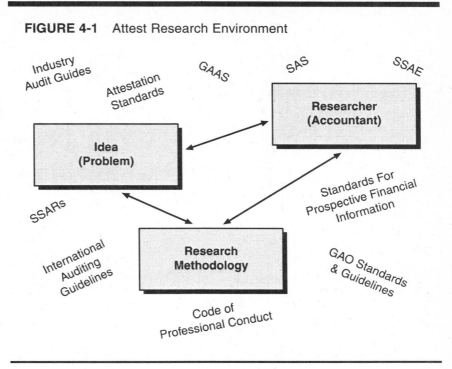

Auditing Standards (GAAS) to these attest services. These services have included the following examples: reporting on descriptions of the client's system of internal controls; reporting to the client on which computer system is the cheapest or has the most capabilities; reporting on insurance claims data; reporting on compliance with regulatory requirements; or reporting on prospective financial statements. More specifically, Wilson Sporting Goods had requested an accounting firm to attest to the statement that Wilson's Ultra golf ball outdistanced its competitors! Consequently, the AICPA has issued *Statements on Standards for Attestation Engagements, Statements on Standards for Accounting and Review Services* , and *Statements on Standards for Accountants' Services on Prospective Financial Information* to provide a general framework and set reasonable guidelines for an attest function in addition to the audit function in order to be responsive to a changing environment and demands of society.

The broad guidelines for an attest engagement have been issued by the Auditing Standards Board (ASB) in conjunction with the Accounting and Review Services Committee and the Management Consulting Services Executive Committee of the AICPA. As listed in Figure 4-3, these attestation standards do not supersede any existing standards but are considered a natural extension of

FIGURE 4-2   Attest Engagments and Guidelines

Attest Engagement:	Guidelines:	Issued by:
Audit	Generally Accepted Audit Standards (GAAS) Statements on Auditing Standards (SASs)	Auditing Standards Board (ASB)
Accounting and Review Services	Statements on Standards for Accounting and Review Services (SSARs)	Accounting and Review Services Committee (ARSC)
Accountant's Services on Prospective Finan- cial Information	Statements on Standards for Accountants' Services on Prospective Financial Information	Auditing Standards Board
Other Attest Services	Statements on Standards for Attestation Engage- ment	ASB, ARSC, and the Management Consulting Ser- vices Executive Committee

the ten generally accepted auditing standards. The design of these attestation standards is such that they provide guidance to the professional to enhance both consistency and quality in the performance of attest services.

Auditing Standard-Setting Environment

In a society where credit is extended widely and business failures occur daily, and where investors wish to study the financial statements of many enterprises, auditing is indispensable. The purpose of the audit report is to add credibility to the financial information. The early development of auditing standards and pro- cedures in the U.S. arose from significant economic upheavals. In 1917 the Fed- eral Reserve Board issued the first audit guideline, entitled "A Memorandum on Balance Sheet Audits," a result of the credit crises during the early 1900s. Later,

FIGURE 4-3   Attestation Standards

General Standards

1. The engagement shall be performed by a practitioner or practitioners having adequate technical training and proficiency in the attest function.
2. The engagement shall be performed by a practitioner or practitioners having adequate knowledge in the subject matter of the assertion.
3. The practitioner shall perform an engagement only if he or she has reason to believe that the following two conditions exist:
   • The assertion is capable of evaluation against reasonable criteria that either have been established by a recognized body or are stated in the presentation of the assertion in sufficiently clear and comprehensive manner for a knowledgeable reader to be able to understand them.
   • The assertion is capable of reasonably consistent estimation or measurement using such criteria.
4. In all matters relating to the engagement, an independence in mental attitude shall be maintained by the practitioner or practitioners.
5. Due professional care shall be exercised in the performance of the engagement.

Standards of Field Work

1. The work shall be adequately planned, and assistants, if any, shall be properly supervised.
2. Sufficient evidence shall be obtained to provide a reasonable basis for the conclusion that is expressed in the report.

Standards of Reporting

1. The report on an engagement shall identify the assertion being reported on and state the character of the engagement.
2. The report shall state the practitioner's conclusion about whether the assertion is presented in conformity with the established or stated criteria against which it was measured.
3. The report shall state all of the practitioner's significant reservations about the engagement and the presentation of the assertion.
4. The report on the engagement to evaluate an assertion that has been prepared in conformity with agreed-upon criteria or on an engagement to apply agreed-upon procedures should contain a statement limiting its use to the parties who have agreed upon such criteria or procedures.

Source: AICPA *Professional Standards,* Vol. 1 (Chicago: Commerce Clearing House), AT Section 100.

the stock market crash and the ensuing depression led to the creation of the Securities and Exchange Commission and prompted the New York Stock Exchange to require that listed companies be audited. Throughout these years, the AICPA has been involved actively in the development of auditing standards and procedures. The general environment within which any given audit is conducted is a very dynamic one and is constantly evolving as the various factors impact the audit process.

The role of the independent auditor can be described as a secondary communication function, wherein an opinion is expressed on financial information reported by management. A primary concern of the auditor, therefore, is whether the client's financial statements are presented in accordance with generally accepted accounting principles. The auditor must also conduct audits in a manner that conforms to auditing standards and procedures and take actions that are guided by professional ethical standards. Additionally, in non-audit engagements the accountant must be aware of attestation standards, statements dealing with compilation and review services, as well as standards for accountants' services on prospective financial information, (i.e., forecasts and projections).

Auditing Standards

Auditing standards differ from auditing procedures in that standards provide measures of the quality of performance, whereas audit procedures refer to the acts or steps to be performed in an engagement. Auditing standards do not vary. They remain identical for all audits. Auditing procedures change, depending on the nature and type of entity under audit and the complexity of the audit.

In contrast to generally accepted accounting principles, which cannot be identified with exactness, the AICPA has formally adopted ten broad requirements for auditors to follow in examining financial statements. These ten requirements, referred to as the ten *Generally Accepted Auditing Standards* (GAAS), are listed in Figure 4-4. In addition to the issuance of the generally accepted auditing standards, the AICPA publishes a series of *Statements on Auditing Standards* (SASs). These statements supplement and interpret the ten generally accepted standards by clarifying audit procedures or prescribing the form and content of the auditor's report. These SASs serve as the primary auditor support in conducting an examination and are a major source of authoritative information when conducting auditing research.

Various forms of the generally accepted auditing standards are also recognized by governmental and internal auditors. The General Accounting Office (GAO), through the comptroller general of the United States, has issued *Governmental Auditing Standards*. The Institute of Internal Auditors has issued *Standards for the Professional Practice of Internal Auditing* under which internal auditors operate. These and other standards are discussed later in this chapter.

FIGURE 4-4   Generally Accepted Auditing Standards

General Standards

1. The examination is to be performed by a person or persons having adequate technical training and proficiency as an auditor.
2. In all matters relating to the assignment, an independence in mental attitude is to be maintained by the auditor or auditors.
3. Due professional care shall be exercised in the performance of the audit and the preparation of the report.

Standards of Field Work

1. The work is to be adequately planned, and assistants, if any, are to be properly supervised.
2. A sufficient understanding of the internal control structure is to be obtained to plan the audit and to determine the nature, timing, and extent of test to be performed.
3. Sufficient competent evidential matter is to be obtained through inspection, observation, inquiries, and confirmations to afford a reasonable basis for an opinion regarding the financial statements under audit.

Standards of Reporting

1. The report shall state whether the financial statements are presented in accordance with generally accepted accounting principles.
2. The report shall identify those circumstances in which such principles have not been consistently observed in the current period in relation to the preceding period.
3. Informative disclosures in the financial statements are to be regarded as reasonably adequate unless otherwise stated in the report.
4. The report shall contain either an expression of opinion regarding the financial statements, taken as a whole, or an assertion to the effect that an opinion cannot be expressed. When an overall opinion cannot be expressed, the reasons therefore should be stated. In all cases where an auditor's name is associated with financial statements, the report should contain a clear-cut indication of the character of the auditor's work and the degree of responsibility the auditor is taking.

Source: AICPA *Professional Standards,* Vol. 1 (Chicago: Commerce Clearing House), AT Section 150.

Auditing Standard-Setting Process

Concern has always existed as to who should set auditing standards for the independent auditor. Prior to establishment of the SEC, Congress debated having audits conducted by a corps of governmental auditors. However, federal chartering of auditors did not take place, and to this day the auditing standard-setting process for independent audits remains in the private sector under the auspices of the AICPA's present senior technical committee on auditing standards—the Auditing Standards Board (ASB).

The establishment and issuance of auditing standards has traditionally been the responsibility of the AICPA. Its Committee on Auditing Procedure (CAP) was formed on January 30, 1939, and functioned until 1972, issuing a series of 54 *Statements on Auditing Procedure,* which were to serve as guidelines for the independent auditor in the exercise of professional judgment on the application of auditing procedures.

In November 1972, the Statements on Auditing Procedure were codified in *Statement on Auditing Standards No. 1,* "Codification of Auditing Standards and Procedures." At this time, the AICPA reorganized its auditing section and changed the name of the committee to the Auditing Standards Executive Committee (AudSEC) and created the Auditing Standards Division within the AICPA. AudSEC served as the AICPA's senior technical committee with the charge of interpreting generally accepted auditing standards and responsibility for issuing Statements on Auditing Standards (SASs). These statements have been incorporated into the AICPA's looseleaf service, *Professional Standards,* which provides a continuous codification of Statements on Auditing Standards.

As a result of the recommendations of the Commission on Auditors' Responsibilities—an independent study group appointed by the AICPA in 1974 to study the structure of the auditing standard-setting process—the AICPA restructured its auditing committee in May, 1978. In October, 1978, a 15-member Auditing Standards Board (ASB) was formed as the successor to AudSEC on all auditing matters and is the present body authorized to issue Statements on Auditing Standards. The Board was given the following charge:

> The AICPA Auditing Standards Board shall be responsible for the promulgation of auditing standards and procedures to be observed by members of the AICPA in accordance with the Institute's rules of conduct.
>
> The board shall be alert to new opportunities for auditors to serve the public, both by the assumption of new responsibilities and by improved ways of meeting old ones, and shall as expeditiously as possible develop standards and procedures that will enable the auditor to assume those responsibilities.

Auditing standards and procedures promulgated by the board shall—

a. Define the nature and extent of the auditor's responsibilities.
b. Provide guidance to the auditor in carrying out his duties, enabling him to express an opinion on the reliability of the representations on which he is reporting.
c. Make special provisions, where appropriate, to meet the needs of small enterprises.
d. Have regard to the costs which they impose on society in relation to the benefits reasonably expected to be derived from the audit function.

The auditing standards board shall provide auditors with all possible guidance in the implementation of its pronouncements, by means of interpretations of its statements, by the issuance of guidelines, and by other means available to it.[3]

In addition, the staff of the Auditing Standards Division of the AICPA has been authorized to issue auditing interpretations on the application of pronouncements (SASs) of the Auditing Standards Board. The interpretations are not to be considered as authoritative as a Statement on Auditing Standards. However, members need to be aware that they may have to justify any departure from an interpretation issued by the Auditing Standards Division of the AICPA. Other publications of the Auditing Standards Division include a number of Industry Audit Guides and Statements of Position. Figure 4-5 presents an overview of the current hierarchy of authoritative auditing support. The auditor should be aware of each of the sources listed, particularly the Statements on Auditing Standards. Figure 4-6 presents a listing of the current existing Audit and Accounting Guides.

The current standard-setting process of the ASB is somewhat similar to that of the FASB:

1. A specific auditing problem or issue is identified.
2. A task force may be established to conduct research on the problem or issue.
3. Public meetings are held to discuss the auditing issue.
4. An exposure draft of a proposed Statement on Auditing Standards may be issued for public comment.
5. A final pronouncement, Statement on Auditing Standards, is issued.

Due to changing economic conditions, the AICPA's Auditing Standards Division currently issues *Audit Risk Alerts* on a periodic basis. These statements

---

3 AICPA *Professional Standards,* Vol. 1 (Chicago: Commerce Clearing House), Appendix A.

FIGURE 4-5   Auditing Authoritative Support

Primary Authoritative Support

A. General Application
1. Generally Accepted Auditing Standards
2. Statements on Auditing Standards
3. Auditing Interpretations
4. AICPA Code of Conduct
5. International Auditing Guidelines

B. Special Application to Certain Entities
1. Industry Audit Guides
2. Statements of Position of the Auditing Standards Division
3. GAO—Government Auditing Standards

Secondary Authoritative Support

A. Audit Research Monographs
B. AICPA Audit and Accounting Manual
C. Journal articles and textbooks

---

provide auditors with an overview of recent economic conditions as well as new professional developments that may have an impact on the audits they perform. Although these documents have not been approved, disapproved, or otherwise acted upon by the ASB, they do provide valuable audit guidance for the auditor.

Unlike an audit that expresses whether the financial statements are in conformity with GAAP, the accountant's examination of prospective financial statements provide assurance only as to whether (1) the prospective financial statements conform to the AICPA's guidelines, and (2) the assumptions used in the projections provide a reasonable basis for a forecast or projection. The accountant must keep in mind that any type of attest service provided must be accompanied by a report as described in the various attestation and auditing standards.

Code of Professional Conduct

A distinguishing mark of any profession is the establishment and acceptance of a code of professional conduct. This code, which is imposed by a profession upon its membership, outlines a minimum level of conduct that is mandatory and enforceable. Such a code of ethics emphasizes the profession's responsibility to the public as well as to colleagues. Every CPA in the practice of public accounting

FIGURE 4-6 AICPA Audit and Accounting Guides

Audit Sampling
Audits of Agriculture Producers and Agriculture Cooperatives
Audits of Airlines
Audits of Banks
Audits of Brokers and Dealers in Securities
Audits of Casinos
Audits of Certain Nonprofit Organizations
Audits of Colleges and Universities
Audits of Credit Unions
Audits of Employee Benefit Plans
Audits of Entities with Oil and Gas Producing Activities
Audits of Federal Government Contractors
Audits of Finance Companies
Audits of Investment Companies
Audits of Property and Liability Insurance Companies
Audits of Providers of Health Care Services
Audits of Savings Institutions
Audits of Service-Center-Produced Records
Audits of State and Local Governmental Units
Audits of Stock Life Insurance Companies
Audits of Voluntary Health and Welfare Organizations
Common Interest Realty Associations
Consideration of Internal Control Structures in a Financial Statement Audit
Construction Contractors
Guide for Prospective Financial Statements
Guide for the Use of Real Estate Appraisal Information
Personal Financial Statements Guide

should be familiar with the code and its applicability to audit, tax, and management advisory services. The AICPA Code of Professional Conduct consists of two main sections, Principles and Rules.

The Principles serve as the basic framework for the Rules, which are mandatory and enforceable. Periodically, the Executive Committee of the Professional Ethics Division of the AICPA issues ethics rulings and interpretations for the purpose to clarify the Code. The Interpretations render guidance to the accountant as to the scope and applicability of the rules. The Rulings help to clarify specific situations confronted by the accountant. Figure 4-7 depicts the hierarchy of these components.

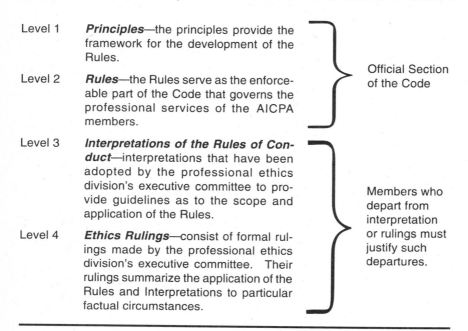

FIGURE 4-7   Hierarchy of the AICPA's Code of Professional Conduct

Level 1   *Principles*—the principles provide the framework for the development of the Rules.

Level 2   *Rules*—the Rules serve as the enforceable part of the Code that governs the professional services of the AICPA members.

}   Official Section of the Code

Level 3   *Interpretations of the Rules of Conduct*—interpretations that have been adopted by the professional ethics division's executive committee to provide guidelines as to the scope and application of the Rules.

Level 4   *Ethics Rulings*—consist of formal rulings made by the professional ethics division's executive committee. Their rulings summarize the application of the Rules and Interpretations to particular factual circumstances.

}   Members who depart from interpretation or rulings must justify such departures.

Departure from the Rules may result in disciplinary action unless the departure can be justified in the circumstances. Disciplinary action may lead to suspension or termination of AICPA membership. Furthermore, a violation of professional conduct may result in revocation of a CPA certificate or license to practice by a state board of accountancy; in many cases, the revocation is sanctioned by the Securities and Exchange Commission. The AICPA's Code of Professional Conduct applies to all members. Certain rules, however, are specifically applicable to the independent auditor. Rule 202 requires compliance with the standards and is stated as follows:

> **Rule 202 — Compliance with standards**. A member who performs auditing, review, compilation, management consulting, tax, or other professional services shall comply with standards promulgated by bodies designated by Council.[4]

---

4   AICPA *Professional Standards,* Vol. 2 (Chicago: Commerce Clearing House), ET Section 202.

Rule 203 generally prohibits the auditor from expressing an opinion that financial statements are in conformity with generally accepted accounting principles if the statements contain any departure from the official pronouncements of the Financial Accounting Standards Board or its predecessors. Rule 203 is stated as follows:

> **Rule 203 — Accounting principles**. A member shall not (1) express an opinion or state affirmatively that the financial statements or other financial data of any entity are presented in conformity with generally accepted accounting principles or (2) state that he or she is not aware of any material modifications that should be made to such statements or data in order for them to be in conformity with generally accepted accounting principles, if such statements contain any departure from an accounting principle promulgated by bodies designated by Council to establish such principles that has a material effect on the statements taken as a whole. If, however, the statements or data contain such a departure and the member can demonstrate that due to unusual circumstances the financial statements would otherwise have been misleading, the member can comply with the rule by describing the departure, its approximate effects, if practicable, and the reasons why compliance with the principle would result in a misleading statement.[5]

As noted in the above two rules, it is important to emphasize that the CPA must comply with generally accepted auditing standards and also be familiar with generally accepted accounting principles when expressing an opinion. Therefore, the practitioner, too, should master a research methodology in order to determine if the audit is in compliance with GAAS and the entity is following GAAP.

Rule 203 was clarified with the issuance of the following two Interpretations:

Interpretations under Rule 203—Accounting principles:

203-1—Departures from established accounting principles. Rule 203 was adopted to require compliance with accounting principles promulgated by the body designated by Council to establish such principles. There is a strong presumption that adherence to officially established accounting principles would in nearly all instances result in financial statements that are not misleading.

---

5   AICPA *Professional Standards,* Vol. 2 (Chicago: Commerce Clearing House), ET Section 203.

However, in the establishment of accounting principles it is difficult to anticipate all of the circumstances to which such principles might be applied. This rule therefore recognizes that upon occasion there may be unusual circumstances where the literal application of pronouncements on accounting principles would have the effect of rendering financial statements misleading. In such cases, the proper accounting treatment is that which will render the financial statements not misleading.

The question of what constitutes unusual circumstances as referred to in Rule 203 is a matter of professional judgment involving the ability to support the position that adherence to a promulgated principle would be regarded generally by reasonable men as producing a misleading result.

Examples of events which may justify departures from a principle are new legislation or the evolution of a new form of business transaction. An unusual degree of materiality or existence of conflicting industry practices are examples of circumstances which would not ordinarily be regarded as unusual in the context of Rule 203.

203-2 — Status of FASB interpretations. Council is authorized under Rule 203 to designate a body to establish accounting principles and has designated the Financial Accounting Standards Board as such body. Council also has resolved that FASB Statements of Financial Accounting Standards, together with those Accounting Research Bulletins and APB Opinions which are not superseded by action of the FASB, constitute accounting principles as contemplated in Rule 203.

In determining the existence of a departure from an accounting principle established by a Statement of Financial Accounting Standards, Accounting Research Bulletin or APB Opinion encompassed by Rule 203, the division of professional ethics will construe such Statement, Bulletin or Opinion in the light of any interpretations thereof issued by the FASB.[6]

Auditing in the Public Sector

Until the early 1970s, there was little interest in whether governmental auditors adhered to auditing standards in auditing a governmental entity. However, as

---

6 AICPA *Professional Standards,* Vol. 2 (Chicago: Commerce Clearing House), ET Section 203.

public sector spending accelerated, legislators, government officials, and the general public became increasingly concerned about how their money was spent and whether government was achieving its goals funded by public dollars. Associated with these concerns was the desire that standards for governmental auditing be established as guidelines for the governmental auditor. To a large degree, the standards and guidelines used in a governmental audit are similar to auditing requirements in the corporate sector. Federal, state, and local governments have placed substantial reliance on the auditing requirements of the AICPA's Auditing Standards Division. However, specific governmental audit concerns have been addressed by various governmental regulatory bodies.

In 1972, the Comptroller General of the United States issued the first major governmental auditing publication, entitled *Standards for Audit of Governmental Organizations, Programs, Activities and Functions* (revised in 1981). These standards, applicable to all governmental organizations, programs, activities, and functions, have the objective of improving the quality of governmental audits at the federal, state, and local levels. These governmental standards were founded on the premise that governmental accountability should focus not only on which funds have been spent, but also the manner and effectiveness of the expenditures. Therefore, these standards provide for an audit scope to include financial and compliance auditing as well as auditing for economy, efficiency, and effectiveness of program results. In 1994, the GAO revised and reissued its auditing publication entitled *Government Auditing Standards*. Federal legislation requires that these GAO auditing standards be followed by federal inspector generals. Also, these standards are audit criteria for federal executive departments and agencies.

Other major audit guidelines for nonprofit organizations issued since 1972 are listed in Figure 4-8. Of major importance has been the issuance of The Single Audit Act of 1984 (Public Law 98-502), which incorporated the concept of an entity-wide financial and compliance "single audit." This Act requires an annual audit of any state or local government unit that receives Federal financial assistance. The single audit concept thus eliminates the need for separate financial and compliance audits conducted by various federal agencies from whom the entity has received funding. By Congressional directive, the Director of the Office of Management and Budget has been given the authority to establish policy and guidelines and the mechanisms to implement single, coordinated financial and compliance audits of grant recipients on a government-wide basis.

Accounting Services

In response to the needs of nonpublic clients,[7] regulatory agencies, and the investing public, the public accounting profession offers compilation or review

---

7   The distinction between a public versus nonpublic client is based on whether the entity's securities are traded publicly on a stock exchange or in the over-the-counter market.

FIGURE 4-8   Major Guidelines for Public Sector Auditing

GAO   (General Accounting Office)
            Government Auditing Standards ("Yellow Book")

OMB   (Office of Management and Budget)
            "Single Audit Act"

AICPA   (American Institute of CPAs)
            Attestation Standards
            Generally Accepted Auditing Standards (GAAS)
            Audit Guides: Audits of Certain Nonprofit Organizations
                           Audits of Colleges and Universities
                           Audits of Federal Government Contractors
                           Audits of State and Local Governmental Units
                           Audits of Voluntary Health and Welfare Organizations

            Statements of Position

---

services to clients rather than conducting an audit examination in accordance with GAAS. A compilation or a review of financial statements are defined as follows:

> Compilation—a service presenting, in the form of financial statements, information that is the representation of management without undertaking to express any assurance on the statements.

> Review—a service performing inquiry and analytical procedures that provide the accountant with a reasonable basis for expressing limited assurance that there are no material modifications that should be made to the statements in order for them to be in conformity with generally accepted accounting principles or, if applicable, with another comprehensive basis of accounting.[8]

Therefore, the basic distinction between these two services is that a review service provides *limited* assurance about the reliability of unaudited financial data presented by management, whereas a compilation engagement provides *no* assurance as to the reliability of the data since the CPA only prepares financial

---

8 Accounting and Review Services Committee, *Statement on Standards for Accounting and Review Services No. 1,* "Compilation and Review of Financial Statements," AICPA, 1978.

statements from information supplied by management in order to obtain more accurate and reliable statements. The CPA is not required to verify this information furnished by the client and therefore provides no assurance regarding the validity of this information.

Guidance for the public accountant for these services has been established by the Accounting and Review Services Committee of the AICPA with the issuance of Statements on Standards for Accounting and Review Services (SSARS). To date, the committee has issued seven statements:

1. "Compilation and Review of Financial Statements," Dec. 1978.
2. "Reporting on Comparative Financial Statements," Oct. 1979.
3. "Compilation Reports on Financial Statements Included in Certain Prescribed Forms," Dec. 1981.
4. "Communication Between Predecessor and Successor Accountants," Dec. 1981.
5. "Reporting on Compiled Financial Statements," July 1982.
6. "Reporting on Personal Financial Statements Included in Written Financial Plans," Sept. 1986.
7. "Omnibus Statement on Standards for Accounting and Review Services," Nov. 1992.

International Auditing

In October, 1977, the International Federation of Accountants (IFAC) was organized through an agreement signed by 63 accounting bodies representing 49 countries. The IFAC stated that its broad objectives were to develop a worldwide accounting profession with harmonized standards. To meet part of the objective relating to auditing standards, the IFAC established the International Auditing Practices Committee (IAPC) to develop and issue international guidelines on the form and content of audit reports. The purpose of the guidelines is to improve the uniformity of auditing practices throughout the world.

The International Auditing Guidelines apply to every independent audit of financial information regardless of the type or size of the entity under audit. However, within each country, local regulations govern. To the extent that the International Auditing Guidelines conform with the specific country's regulation, the audit will be considered in accordance with the International Auditing Guidelines. In the event that they differ, the members of the IFAC will work towards the implementation of the Guideline, if practicable, within the specific country.

The ASB has specifically addressed the concern of reporting on financial statements prepared for use in other countries through the issuance of Statement on Auditing Standards No. 51, *Reporting on Financial Statements for Use in Other Countries.* This statement provides guidance to the independent auditor practicing in the United States and reporting on financial statements of an American entity that have been prepared in conformity with accounting principles of another country for use outside the U.S. If the financial statements are for use only outside of the U.S., the auditor may use either of the following:

1. An American-style report modified to report on the accounting principles of the particular country, including:
   a. Identity of the financial statements (F/S).
   b. Reference to the note that describes the basis of presentation, including the nationality of GAAP.
   c. Examination made in accordance with U.S. GAAS (and of the other country, if appropriate).
   d. Opinion as to conformity with basis of presentation and consistency.

2. The report form of the other country, provided that:
   a. Such a report would be used by auditors in the other country in similar circumstances.
   b. The auditor understands and can make such attestations.

Since GAAP reports from other countries are generally not useful to U.S. readers, the auditor should consider issuing two reports—one using U.S. GAAP and the other using GAAP from the other country. Such financial statements may receive limited distribution in the U.S. (i.e., the parties have the opportunity to directly discuss the F/S with the entity). However, such financial statements may not receive a general distribution unless:

1. They are accompanied by statements prepared in conformity with U.S. GAAP.
2. The auditor uses an U.S.-type report, qualified for departures from U.S. GAAP.

Subcommittees of the IAPC have been established for the preparation and drafting of audit guidelines on specific subjects determined by the IAPC. After initial preparation, an exposure draft is balloted by the IAPC. If approved by three-quarters of the total voting, the exposure draft is disseminated for review. After the comments and suggestions are reviewed, the IAPC then votes on the issuance of a definitive International Auditing Guideline. To date, 31 guidelines have been issued on various topics ranging from the objective and scope of the financial audit to special purpose reports. (See Appendix A at the end of this chapter.)

Role of Judgment in Accounting and Auditing Research

The accountant or auditor exercises professional judgment in considering whether the substance of business transactions differs from the form, in evaluating the adequacy of disclosure, in assessing the probable impact of future events, and in determining materiality limits. This informed judgment on the part of the practitioner is the foundation of the accounting profession. In providing an attest engagement, the end result is often the rendering of a considered opinion or principled judgment. In effect, the independent accountant gathers relevant and reliable information, evaluates and judges its contents, and then formalizes an opinion on the financial information or statements.

A review of current authoritative literature reveals that certain pronouncements on generally accepted accounting principles disclose specifically which accounting principle is applicable for a given business transaction. Other pronouncements only provide general guidelines and in some cases suggest acceptable alternative principles. The process of applying professional judgment in choosing among alternatives is not carried out in isolation, but through consultation with other professionals knowledgeable in the area. In rendering his/her professional judgment, the accountant/auditor will need to exercise critical-thinking skills in the development of a solution or opinion.

Statement on Auditing Standards No. 5 makes the following point on the use of professional judgment in determining conformity with GAAP:

> .04 The auditor's opinion that financial statements present fairly an entity's financial position, results of operations, and changes in financial position in conformity with generally accepted accounting principles *should be based on his judgment* as to whether
>
> (a) the accounting principles selected and applied have general acceptance;
>
> (b) the accounting principles are appropriate in the circumstances;
>
> (c) the financial statements, including the related notes, are informative of matters that may affect their use, understanding, and interpretation;
>
> (d) the information presented in the financial statements is classified and summarized in a reasonable manner; that is, neither too detailed nor too condensed; and
>
> (e) the financial statements reflect the underlying events and transactions in a manner that presents the financial position, results of operations, and changes in financial position stated within a range of acceptable limits; that is, limits that are reasonable and practicable to attain in financial statements. (Emphasis added)[9]

---

9 AICPA *Professional Standards,* Vol. 1 (Chicago: Commerce Clearing House), AU Section 411.04.

In order to render an opinion based upon professional judgment, the auditor often considers the opinions of other professionals. In such cases, the practitioner can use several published sources to determine how others have dealt with specific accounting and reporting applications of GAAP. The AICPA publishes *Technical Practice Aids,* which contains the "Technical Information Service." This service consists of inquiries and replies that describe an actual problem that was encountered in practice and the interpretation and recommendations that were provided along with relevant standards and other authoritative sources. Chapter 5 includes a detailed discussion of *Technical Practice Aids.*

Economic Consequences

Since time is a scarce commodity, the auditor should weigh the cost/benefit tradeoffs in extending the research process. The researcher should address the problem until all reasonable doubt relating to the issue has been eliminated, recognizing the hidden costs of making an improper audit decision. Besides the legal damages from an association with a negligent audit, the auditor can face criminal penalties; FTC, SEC, and other government sanctions; loss of reputation among the auditor's peers; and a significant loss of the auditor's existing clients in a competitive environment.

Other Reference Sources

The AICPA also provides other reference sources for the practitioner to use in determining how to apply accounting principles. *Accounting Trends & Techniques* is an annual publication designed to illustrate current reporting practices and chart significant trends in these practices. *Financial Reporting Surveys* consist of a continuing series of studies designed to show in detail how specific accounting and reporting questions are actually being handled. The National Automated Accounting Research System (NAARS) is a full-text, computer-based information retrieval system. Among the information stored by this system are the annual reports of over 4,000 publicly traded corporations. These research tools are discussed in detail in Chapter 6. The practitioner can use these references to determine current accounting and reporting practices. With the use of information gathered, and through consultation with other accountants, a decision may be reached on the appropriate accounting principle to be used for the transaction being researched or the auditing issue under investigation.

Summary

This chapter has presented an overview of the attestation standard-setting environment, accounting services, and professional ethics. Familiarity with this information, in particular the authoritative pronouncements that exist, will aid the practitioner in the research process.

In researching an accounting or auditing issue, the practitioner will be called upon to use professional judgment in the decision-making process. Experience is undoubtedly the primary factor in developing good professional judgment. However, subsequent chapters present a research methodology that should aid in the application of professional judgment.

Discussion Questions

1. Define an attest engagement.

2. Identify three other attest services in addition to the normal financial statement audit.

3. Differentiate between auditing standards and attestation standards.

4. What guidelines exist for the performance of accounting and review services?

5. Differentiate between auditing standards and auditing procedures.

6. Discuss the relationship between generally accepted auditing standards (GAAS) and Statements on Auditing Standards (SAS).

7. Discuss the applicability of the first and third general standards of GAAS to accounting and auditing research.

8. Discuss the historical relationship of the Auditing Standards Board, Auditing Standards Executive Committee, and Committee on Auditing Procedure. Also, list the authoritative pronouncements issued by each body.

9. State the objective of the Single Audit Act. When is this act applicable?

10. List the primary auditing guidelines for public sector auditing.

11. Explain the importance of the Code of Professional Conduct in the performance of an audit.

12. Explain the significance of Rules 202 and 203 of the AICPA's Code of Professional Conduct.

13. How may accounting or auditing research aid the practitioner in complying with Rules 202 and 203 of the Code of Professional Conduct?

14. What role does professional judgment play in the daily activities of the accountant or auditor?

15. What authoritative auditing literature that has general applicability in practice is considered primary authoritative support?

16. What guidelines are available for the accountant in serving the needs of the nonpublic client?

17. What authoritative body exists as to the development of international auditing standards?

Appendix A
Selected Pronouncements Issued By IFAC

International Auditing Guidelines

IAG	1.	Objective and Scope of the Audit of Financial Statements
IAG	2.	Audit Engagement Letters
IAG	3.	Basic Principles Governing an Audit
IAG	4.	Planning
IAG	5.	Using the Work of Another Auditor
IAG	6.	Study and Evaluation of the Accounting System and Related Internal Controls in Connection with an Audit
IAG	7.	Control of the Quality of Audit Work
IAG	8.	Audit Evidence
IAG	9.	Documentation
IAG	10.	Using the Work of an Internal Auditor
IAG	11.	Fraud and Error
IAG	12.	Analytical Review
IAG	13.	The Auditor's Report on Financial Statements
IAG	14.	Other Information in Documents Containing Audited Financial Statements
IAG	15.	Auditing in an EDP Environment
IAG	16.	Computer-Assisted Audit Techniques
IAG	17.	Related Parties
IAG	18.	Using the Work of an Expert
IAG	19.	Audit Sampling
IAG	20.	The Effects of an EDP Environment on the Study and Evaluation of the Accounting System and Related Internal Controls
IAG	21.	Date of the Auditor's Report; Events After the Balance Sheet Date; Discovery of Facts After the Financial Statements Have Been Issued
IAG	22.	Representations by Management
IAG	23.	Going Concern
IAG	24.	Special Purpose Audit Reports
IAG	25.	Materiality and Audit Risk
IAG	26.	Audit of Accounting Estimates
IAG	27.	The Examination of Prospective Financial Information
IAG	28.	First Year Audit Engagements—Opening Balances
IAG	30.	Knowledge of the Business
IAG	31.	Consideration of Laws and Regulations in an Audit of Financial Statements International Auditing Guidelines/Related Services

C H A P T E R   5

SOURCES OF AUTHORITATIVE LITERATURE

Learning Objectives

After completing this chapter, you should understand:

- The main sources of authoritative literature on accounting principles and auditing standards.

- How to use the *Index to Accounting and Auditing Technical Pronouncements* (IAATP).

- How to gather evidence from the AICPA *Professional Standards,* the FASB *Accounting Standards,* and the AICPA *Technical Practice Aids.*

- The basic format of APB Opinions and FASB and GASB Statements.

A major component of the research process is the review of the pertinent accounting or auditing literature. This chapter outlines the overall structure of the authoritative literature, with an emphasis on developing the technical skills required to access the AICPA *Professional Standards* and the FASB *Accounting Standards* series, which are the most comprehensive sources of authoritative accounting and auditing literature.

Many of the techniques used to access the AICPA or the FASB Standards series, such as the keyword index, are also applicable to pronouncements of other rule-making bodies. In addition to the AICPA and the FASB, the Cost Accounting Standards Board (CASB), the Governmental Accounting Standards Board (GASB), and the U.S. Securities and Exchange Commission (SEC) produce publications stating their official positions on various accounting issues. These organizations also publish unofficial interpretations and descriptive surveys to help the practitioner implement required accounting principles. The identification and use of these unofficial publications are also discussed.

Many research sources are available to aid the researcher in the quest for a solution to a particular problem or issue. A summary of the various sources of authoritative literature on accounting principles and auditing standards is shown in Figure 5-1.

Accessing the Authoritative Literature

As can be seen from the previous section, there are many sources of authoritative accounting and auditing literature. The publications presented in Figure 5-2, page 104, are among the researcher's most valuable tools for identifying and locating authoritative literature in the specific area under investigation. These research services enable the practitioner to keep abreast of the pronouncements, interpretations, and guidelines that govern today's technical and professional activities. The publications and techniques for using them to conduct efficient research are discussed in the following sections.

Sound research techniques rest on these basic principles:

1. *The order of search is important.* Searches should begin with sources that encompass a broad range of pronouncements and only then move to narrower sources (those that contain specific pronouncements). Remember that primary authoritative support should be consulted first followed by secondary sources, if necessary. Otherwise, the researcher may overlook major material.
2. *Sources are systems.* That is, they are more than lists, and the researcher should seek their systematic aid. Many sources, for example, cross-reference items in order to guide the researcher to the most productive main terms (terms that may never have occurred to the researcher).

FIGURE 5-1   Sources of Authoritative Literature

1. Pronouncements of authoritative bodies that prescribe accounting principles that must be followed in order for the financial statements to be considered in conformity with generally accepted accounting principles.

Authoritative Body/Title of Literature

AICPA:
- Committee on Accounting Procedures (CAP)/*Accounting Research Bulletins (ARBs)*
- Committee on Terminology/*Accounting Terminology Bulletins*
- Accounting Principles Board (APB)/*APB Opinions*

Cost Accounting Standards Board (CASB)/*Cost Accounting Standards (CASs)/ Interpretations*

Financial Accounting Federation (FAF):
- Financial Accounting Standards Board (FASB)/*Statements of Financial Accounting Standards (SFASs)/ Interpretations*
- Consensus of Emerging Issues Task Force (EITF)
- National Council on Governmental Accounting (NCGA)/*Statements/ Interpretations*
- Governmental Accounting Standards Board (GASB)/*Statements of Governmental Accounting Standards (GASs)*

Securities and Exchange Commission (SEC)
  / *Regulation S-K*
  / *Regulation S-X*
  / *Accounting Series Releases (ASRs)*
  / *Financial Reporting Release (FRRs)*
  / *Accounting and Auditing Enforcement Releases (AAERs)*

2. Authoritative literature that is considered descriptive of generally accepted accounting principles, but does not prescribe such principles.

Authoritative Body/Title of Literature

AICPA:
- Special Committees/*Industry Accounting Guides*
- Accounting Standards Division/*Statements of Position*

3. Literature that unofficially interprets pronouncements of authoritative bodies.

Authoritative Body/Title of Literature

AICPA: Accounting Principles Board (APB)/*APB Interpretations*

FAF: Financial Accounting Standards Board (FASB)/*Technical Bulletins*

Securities and Exchange Commission (SEC)/*Staff Accounting Bulletins (SABs)*

FIGURE 5-1 (continued)

4. Authoritative literature that expresses views on accounting theory rather than specific elements of generally accepted accounting principles.

Authoritative Body/Title of Literature

AICPA: Accounting Principles Board (APB)/*APB Statements*

FAF: Financial Accounting Standards Board (FASB)/*Statements of Financial Accounting Concepts (SFACs)*
- Special Committees/*Industry Accounting Guides*
- Accounting Standards Division/*Statements of Position*

5. Authoritative literature on auditing standards.

Authoritative Body/Title of Literature

AICPA:
- Auditing Standards Division
  / *Statement on Auditing Standards (SASs)*
  / *Auditing Interpretations*
  / *Industry Audit Guides*
  / *Statements of Position*
- Professional Ethics Division/*Code of Professional Conduct*

Index to Accounting and Auditing Technical Pronouncements (IAATP).

This guide, published annually by the staff of the AICPA, is a cumulative index of both authoritative and semi-authoritative sources of accounting and auditing pronouncements. It provides access to the pronouncements of the following authoritative bodies:

1. American Institute of Certified Public Accountants
2. Cost Accounting Standards Board
3. Financial Accounting Standards Board
4. Governmental Accounting Standards Board
5. International Accounting Standards Committee
6. International Federation of Accountants
7. National Council on Governmental Accounting
8. Securities and Exchange Commission

The index coordinates information from all sources of accounting and auditing technical pronouncements. Thus, the researcher is assured that all authoritative pronouncements on a topic have been reviewed.

FIGURE 5-2 Primary Research Publications

AICPA Index to Accounting and Auditing Technical Pronouncements

Index to pronounce-
ments of the AICPA,
FASB, SEC, GASB,
and other professional
and regulatory bodies

GASB Codifi-
cation of
Government
Accounting &
Financial
Reporting
Studies

- GASB Statements,
  Interpretations,
  Technical Bulletins,
  and Concept
  Statements
- Statements and
  Interpretations of
  the National
  Council on
  Governmental
  Accounting
- AICPA—Audits of
  State and Local
  Governmental
  Units, and
  Statements of
  Position

AICPA
Professional
Standards
Volume 1 / Volume 2

- U.S. Auditing
  Standards
- Accounting and
  Review Services
- Code of Professional
  Conduct
- AICPA Bylaws
- International
  Accounting
- International Auditing
- Management
  Advisory Services
- Quality Control
- Tax Practice

U.S.
Comptroller
General
"Yellow Book"

- Standards for Audit
  of Governmental
  Organizations,
  Programs,
  Activities, and
  Functions

FASB
Professional
Standards
Original Pronouncements / Current Text

- FASB Statements,
  Interpretations, and
  Technical Bulletins
- APB Opinions,
  Statements, and
  Interpretations
- Accounting Research
  Bulletins
- Accounting Technol-
  ogy Bulletins

Congress
"Single-
Audit Act
— 1984"

- Requirements of
  a single
  coordinated audit
  of the aggregate
  federal financial
  assistance
  provided to a
  governmental
  unit during its
  fiscal year

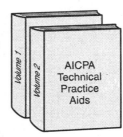

AICPA
Technical
Practice
Aids
Volume 1 / Volume 2

- Technical Information
  Service
- Statements of Posi-
  tion of the Accounting
  Standards Division
- Statements of Posi-
  tion of the Auditing
  Standards Division
- Voluntary Quality
  Control Review
  Program

The general format of the index, which consists of four segments, is as follows:

(1) MAIN TERM
(2) Cross-references
(3) Index strings
(4) Citations

A sample index entry that illustrates the format is presented in Figure 5-3.

The *main terms* are keywords drawn from a specially designed comprehensive list of accounting and auditing terms. Following the main term is a cross-reference listing of terms associated with the main term. Cross-references are coded BT (broader term), NT (narrower term), or RT (related term). There is a UF (used for) code that indicates synonyms for the main term, and a U (use) code that indicates that the cross-reference term is used as the main term for citations in the index. The user can broaden or narrow the scope of the search by selecting terms listed as cross-references.

Following the cross-references is a series of index strings that convey the subject matter of pronouncements relating to the main term. A citation for each pronouncement appears to the right of the index string. The citation is an alphanumeric code that indicates the source of the pronouncement, its number, and, if applicable, the section and paragraph number location within the reference sources.

FIGURE 5-3   Entry from *Index to Accounting and Auditing Technical Pronouncements*

Audit Planning and Supervision	(Main term)
BT Auditing standards)	
BT Field work standards)	
BT GAAS (standards))	(Cross-references)
BT Planning and supervision)	
RT Analytical review procedures)	
RT Audit scope)	
RT Professional skepticism)	
Governmental accounting . . . Auditing procedure, Audit scope: Internal control structures, Compliance testing, Analytical procedures, Audit programs, Representation letters, Legal letters, Disclosure, Accountants independence [index string]	AAG-SLG 3.24 [Citation]
Field work standards, Audit administration techniques . . . Audit scope and Audit programs, Auditing procedures and Internal control evaluation [index string]	SAS 22/311 [Citation]

The reader should obtain a copy of the index and become familiar with its use. There are exercises at the end of this chapter designed to provide practice on the use of the index. The reader should be aware of the *keyword* concept used as a foundation for organizing the index. The keywords that are used to access the index are developed in the problem-definition stage of the research process. However, the index can also be useful in refining the statement of the problem.

AICPA Professional Standards.

The *Professional Standards* series is available in an annually updated paperback edition or in a two-volume looseleaf subscription service as shown in Figure 5-2. The looseleaf service has the advantage of being continually updated. Volume 1 contains the U.S. auditing standards. Figure 5-4 shows the major divisions including the subdivisions of the Statement on Auditing Standards (SASs) section and the topics covered in the appendixes. The material within each subdivision is arranged by numbered section, and each paragraph within a section is decimally numbered. References to sections in Volume 1 are preceded by the citation AU. To illustrate the organization and referencing system of the *Professional Standards*, the table of contents of AU Section 200 is reproduced below:

AU Section 200—THE GENERAL STANDARDS

Section		Paragraph
201	Nature of the General Standards	.01
210	Training and Proficiency of the Independent Auditor	.01–.05
220	Independence	.01–.07
230	Due Care in the Performance of Work	.01–.04

The numbering system facilitates references to specific sections or paragraphs within a section. For example, AU Section 210.03 refers to the third paragraph of Section 210.

Another major division in Volume 1 of the *Professional Standards* is Auditing Interpretations. As discussed previously, the Interpretations provide guidance on the application of SASs. Auditing Interpretations are numbered in the 9000 series, with the last three digits specifying the SAS section to which an Interpretation relates. For example, AU Section 9326 indicates that the Interpretation relates to AU Section 326.

Volume 2 contains ten major divisions, which are listed in Figure 5-4, along with the related citations. Within each major division are several subdivisions, which are too numerous to list here. The material within each division is organized by numbered sections and paragraphs in the same manner as Volume 1.

A search for information on a particular subject may begin with the Master Topical Index, which identifies individual indexes containing detailed information.

FIGURE 5-4 Organization of the AICPA *Professional Standards*

VOLUME 1   **Citation**

Statements on Auditing Standards .... AU *Sec.*
    Introduction... 100
    The General Standards 200
    The Standards of Field Work 300
    The First, Second, and Third Standards of Reporting.......... 400
    The Fourth Standard of Reporting....................... 500
    Other Types of Reports 600
    Special Topics 700
    Compliance Auditing 800
Special Reports of the Committee on Auditing Procedures 900
    Auditing Interpretation 9000

Appendixes:

A. Historical Background
B. List of Statements on Auditing Procedure
C. Sources of Sections in Current Text
D. Cross-Reference Tables for Auditing Interpretations
E. AICPA Audit and Accounting Guides and Statements of Position
F. Schedule of Changes in Statements in Auditing Standards
G. AU Sections Superseded by Statements on Auditing Standards
    Number 55

Statements on Standards for Attestation Engagements......... AT *Sec.*
    Attestation Standards................................ 100
    Attestation Standards Interpretations 9100
    Financial Forecasts and Protections 200
    Reporting on Pro Forma Financial Information 300
    Reporting on an Entity's Internal Control Structure Over
        Financial Reporting............................... 400
    Compliance Attestation 500

VOLUME 2   **Citation**

    Accounting and Review Services .... AR
    Code of Professional Conduct .... ET
    Bylaws of the AICPA .... BL
    International Accounting Standards .... AC
    International Standards on Auditing .... AU
    Consulting Services................................. CS
    Quality Control.................................... QC
    Quality Review.................................... QR
    Tax Practice .... TX
    Personal Financial Planning .... PFP

Alternatively, the researcher may go directly to the appropriate detailed index.

FASB Accounting Standards.

Each year, the FASB compiles and publishes accounting standards in two complementary volumes. The first, *Original Pronouncements,* contains the complete original text of APB Opinions, Statements, and Interpretations; AICPA Accounting Research Bulletins; and FASB Statements of Concepts, Statements of Standards, Interpretations, and Technical Bulletins. The pronouncements are arranged in chronological order. All superseded and amended material is printed in a lightly-colored panel to distinguish it from current material.

The other volume, *Current Text*, which is available in a two-volume paperback set or as a two-volume looseleaf service, is organized alphabetically by subject. The material presented under each subject begins with an integrated presentation of all pronouncements covered under Ethics Rule 203 Accounting Principles. Pronouncements not covered by Ethics Rule 203 immediately follow the official text. The reader is advised to note that the *Current Text* does not include dissenting opinions of the board or committee members not in agreement with the original pronouncements. The dissenting opinions can often shed light on the scope and limitations of a pronouncement and can be located in the volume of *Original Pronouncements.*

The *Current Text* is divided by volumes into (1) General Standards, which contains the standards that are applicable to all entities and (2) Industry Standards, which contains the standards applicable only to entities in specific industries. The appendixes to these two volumes contain a cross-reference of the original pronouncements to the *Current Text* paragraphs, a schedule of amended and superseded accounting pronouncements, and the effective dates of the pronouncements.

Each section of the *Current Text* is identified by an alphanumeric code, and paragraphs within each section are decimally numbered. For example, the reference A06.110 refers to Section A06, "Accounting Changes," and paragraph 110. Each volume of the *Current Text* concludes with a comprehensive Topical Index. Exercises at the end of this chapter provide an opportunity to use the *Current Text.*

Technical Practice Aids.

The AICPA publishes two volumes of nonauthoritative examples and commentary under the title of Technical Practice Aids (see Figure 5-2).

Volume 1 contains the Technical Information Service (TIS), which consists of a series of questions and replies. The information is categorized under major headings: Financial Statement Presentation; Assets; Liabilities and Deferred Credits; Capital; Revenue and Expense; Special Industry Problems; Special Organizational Problems; Audit Field Work; and Audit Reports.

The TIS includes inquiries and replies based upon selected Technical Information Service correspondence dealing with various accounting or auditing issues. As a matter of policy, the TIS staff does not render opinions on tax or the legal aspects of questions submitted by practitioners. Additions to the Technical Information Service are initiated by practitioners' questions related to accounting or auditing problems. These questions are then answered by the TIS staff accountants. The responses are not authoritative pronouncements, but are an expression of an expert's professional opinion, supported by reference to authoritative literature if applicable. This service permits the practitioner to communicate directly with the AICPA in attempting to resolve an issue. By reading the questions posed to the TIS, and the TIS staff's previous responses, a researcher can gain insight into how other professionals have interpreted and implemented professional standards. If the particular area has not been presented to the TIS staff, the researcher can submit an inquiry. The information obtained from the TIS can be used by the researcher in forming conclusions and exercising professional judgment.

Each major section is preceded by a table of contents indicating the main topics covered. There are two appendixes concluding Volume 1. The first appendix is a cross-reference index between official pronouncements cited in the volume and the section number where the pronouncement is cited. The second appendix is a keyword topical index to the volume.

Volume 2 contains the Statements of Position (SOPs) of the Accounting Standards Division and the Auditing Standards Division. These SOPs are arranged in chronological order as they are issued. The Accounting Division's SOPs are followed by a keyword topical index. Volume 2 concludes with a listing of the Accounting Standards Division's Practice Bulletins and Issues Papers.

Government Accounting Pronouncements

Beside researching issues in the private sector, the researcher often must research issues in the public area. The not-for-profit arena's share of the country's gross national product has grown significantly, and this trend should continue into the foreseeable future. Thus, similar to the financial arena, Figure 5-2 highlights the three major primary research publications in the governmental arena. First, the *GASB Codification of Government Accounting & Financial Reporting Studies* contains all GASB Statements, Interpretations, Technical Bulletins, and Concept Statements. It also codifies the National Council on Government Accounting's Statements and Interpretations, as well as the AICPA's Audit Guides of State and Local Governments and Statements of Position. The *GASB Codification* corresponds to the private sector's FASB *Accounting Standards.*

Second, the U.S. Comptroller General's "Yellow Book" contains a codification of Audit Standards for Government Organizations, programs, activities, and functions. This text operates much the same as the AICPA *Professional*

Standards. Finally, the U.S. Congress's "Single Audit Act of 1984" requires all state and local government units receiving at least $100,000 of federal assistance per fiscal year to have an audit made in conformity with the standards of this act. Government units receiving between $25,000–$100,000 of such annual assistance may also adhere to the audit requirement of this Act. These audits contain both financial and compliance components and are subject to oversight by federal agencies designated by the United States Office of Management and Budget.

Reading an APB Opinion, FASB Statement, or GASB Statement

In researching an issue, the researcher may be required to read a specific APB Opinion, FASB Statement, or GASB Statement. In such a case, the researcher should be aware that there is a basic format that is followed in the APB Opinions and FASB Statements. Depending upon the complexity of the pronouncement, the following elements may be included: an introduction to the accounting issues addressed by the pronouncement, the background of the business event and accounting issues, the basis of the Board's conclusions, the actual opinion or statement of accounting standard, the effective date to implement the standard, illustrations of application, and the disclosures required. These basic elements are not necessarily presented as separate sections of all Opinions or Statements. Those that are relatively short may combine the introduction and background information and eliminate the illustration of applications section if it is not a complicated principle. However, there is always a separate section designated as the Opinion or Standard of Accounting.

The introductory section defines the accounting issue that has necessitated an authoritative pronouncement. This section gives the scope of the pronouncement; that is, it defines the type of entity affected. It can also limit the application of the pronouncement to companies of specific size. For example, FASB Statement No. 33, which was superseded by FASB Statement 89 with the same title, "Financial Reporting and Changing Prices," is limited to public companies with inventories and fixed assets of $125 million or total assets of a billion dollars. FASB Statement No. 21, "Suspension of the Reporting of Earnings per Share and Segment Information by Non-public Enterprises," specifically limits the application of APB Opinion No. 15, "Earnings per Share," and FASB Statement No. 14, "Segment Reporting," to publicly held corporations. The introduction also gives the effects of the new pronouncement on previously issued standards. It specifies which pronouncements or sections of prior pronouncements are superseded by the new standard. Generally, within the introduction, there is a summary of the standard so that the researcher sees quickly if the standard applies to the specific situation being investigated.

The background information section describes in more detail the business events and related accounting treatments presented in the pronouncement. This section develops the various arguments supporting alternative approaches to resolving the issue. The underlying assumptions for these alternatives are defined, and the different interpretations of the economic impact of the business event are presented. This section follows the introduction in the APB Opinions, while the FASB generally places the background information in an appendix to the official pronouncement.

The basis for conclusion is described in the Opinions and Statements. This section explains the rationale for the accounting principles prescribed in the pronouncement, indicating which arguments were accepted and which were rejected. (Generally, the APB incorporates the basis of conclusion within the Opinion section of the pronouncement. The FASB incorporates dissenting viewpoints at the end of its main section, Standards of Financial Accounting and Reporting, and positions the Basis for Conclusion in a separate appendix.) The background information and basis for conclusion provide the researcher with a description of the business events and transactions covered by the pronouncement. These sections can be helpful in determining if the pronouncement addresses the specific issue under investigation. If the researcher is in the early stages of investigation, these sections can be helpful in defining the business transactions, determining their economic impact, and relating them to the proper reporting format.

The opinion or standard section prescribes the accounting principles that must be applied to the business transactions described in the pronouncement. The length of this section will depend upon the complexity of the business events involved.

The standard section can be very short, as in the case of FASB Statement No. 73, "Reporting a Change in Accounting for Railroad Track Structures," which basically requires the change to depreciation accounting for railroad track structures be applied retroactively, or it can be very long and complicated, as in FASB Statement No. 13, "Accounting for Leases." In Statement No. 13, the board established specialized terminology; set up criteria for distinguishing various types of leases; and established accounting, reporting, and disclosure requirements for the various leases. All of these items are within the standard section. This section represents the heart of the official pronouncement and must be followed when the researcher concludes that the standard applies to the business transactions under investigation.

The effective date section states when the new pronouncement goes into effect. It also gives any transition period that might be used by a company to implement a new standard. For example, FASB Statement No. 13 had a four-year transition period to permit companies to gather data for retroactive application of this complicated pronouncement on lease transactions. If the board prescribes the method of implementation, retroactive restatement, cumulative effect, or prospective application, the method will be indicated in this section of the pronouncement.

Summary

A major task of the researcher is that of reviewing current professional literature in the search for authoritative support. This chapter focused on the sources of authoritative support and semiauthoritative literature, as well as efficient means of accessing the literature for a solution to the issue under investigation. The resources presented include the AICPA's *Index to Accounting and Auditing Technical Pronouncements*, the AICPA's *Professional Standards* and *Technical Practice Aids,* and the FASB *Accounting Standards.* These publications provide the most comprehensive, up-to-date coverage of the current standards in every major area of professional activity plus guidance in applying the standards in practice.

Appendix A to this chapter is a set of exercises that emphasizes the methodology of the literature search step in the research process. Chapters 6 and 7 present additional research tools for your use with a discussion of computerized databases. Also presented in Chapter 6 is a discussion of conducting accounting and auditing research via the Internet. Chapter 8 attempts to refine the research process via a comprehensive problem and additional cases.

Discussion Questions

1. Identify the major research tools (literature sources) that are discussed in this chapter. Also briefly describe the basic contents of each source.

2. What primary research publication would the researcher use to locate:
   a. A FASB Technical Bulletin?
   b. A specific Rule of Conduct in the Code of Professional Conduct?
   c. An auditing Statement of Position?
   d. An Accounting Research Bulletin?

3. Explain the purpose of the *keyword* concept in accounting and/or auditing research.

4. What is the purpose of the AICPA's Technical Information Service?

5. List the major elements or segments of a specific APB Opinion or FASB Statement.

6. Name four authoritative bodies that prescribe accounting principles that act as GAAP.

7. Name four publications that include prescribed accounting principles that act as GAAP.

8. Name the eight authoritative bodies whose pronouncements are contained in the *Index to Accounting and Auditing Technical Pronouncements* (IAATP).

9. Name the four segments of the IAATP that make up its general format.

10. What is meant by the following in the IAATP?
    a. BT
    b. NT
    c. RT
    d. UF
    e. U

11. What concept is used to organize the IAATP?

12. a. Name two of the main divisions of Volume 1 of the AICPA *Professional Standards*.
    b. What is the relationship between the SASs and Section 9000?

13. What are the two volumes published by the FASB annually, and how do they differ?

14. What are the elements of the basic format of APB Opinions and FASB Statements? Describe briefly what is contained in each element.

15. Briefly explain the contents of the "Yellow Book."

APPENDIX A
Exercises

The following exercises emphasize the use of the *Index to Accounting and Auditing Technical Pronouncements*, the *Professional Standards,* and the FASB *Accounting Standards Current Text*. Completion of the exercises should provide a working knowledge of these research tools. The ability to apply these tools will be tested in Chapter 8 in researching various comprehensive problems.

Exercises 1–3 relate to the use of the *Index to Accounting and Auditing Technical Pronouncements*.

1. Identify the authoritative literature indicated by the following citations:
   a. SAS 05/411
   b. ACC-SOP 75-02
   c. AAG-FGC 1.01
   d. SEC ASR 193

2. Explain the relationship of each of the following index components to the others and describe the impact of each on a research effort:
   a. Common Stock Equivalents
   b. UF Residual Securities
   c. BT Securities
   d. NT Warrants (securities)
   e. RT Convertible Preferred Stock

3. Answer the following questions with respect to the keyword *Denial of opinion.*
   a. What main term is used for this keyword?
   b. List a broader term that could be used as a main term reference.
   c. List a narrower term that could be used as a main term reference.
   d. List some terms that are related to this keyword.

Exercises 4–6 relate to the use of the AICPA *Professional Standards.*

4. Identify the original pronouncement indicated by each of the following citations:
   a. AU Section 504
   b. AU Section 333A
   c. AU Section 9508.01
   d. ET Section 301.04

5. Give citations for authoritative literature covering the following topics:
   a. Confirmation of receivables
   b. Effects of illegal acts on auditor's report
   c. Custody of audit working papers
   d. Auditor's standard report

6. Using the *Professional Standards*, locate the authoritative literature addressing the problem presented in the following situation.

    The Press-Punch Corporation is a closely held company (ten major stockholders) that manufactures parts for the three major U.S. auto companies. Two of the major stockholders formed a partnership that owns the building occupied by Press-Punch. The leasing of the building to Press-Punch is the only business activity of the partnership. As the auditor for Press-Punch, you need to determine the financial statement disclosure requirements for this related-party transaction.

Exercises 7–10 relate to the use of the two volumes of FASB *Accounting Standards Current Text.*

7. Identify the source (original pronouncement) for each of the following citations:
    a. I73.125
    b. C51.109
    c. L10.116
    d. D22.509–.513

8. The Comet Powerboat Company manufactures one of the most popular speedboats in the U.S. As an incentive to its dealers to keep an adequate stock in their showrooms, the company allows dealers to return any unsold boats at the end of the boating season. Locate authoritative literature in the *Current Text* that addresses the proper revenue recognition procedure for Comet Powerboat Company, taking into consideration the dealer's right to return.

9. Give the *Current Text* citations for the following keywords:
    a. Pooling-of-interests
    b. Dividend disclosure
    c. Patents
    d. Warranties-revenue recognition
    e. Personal property tax

10. Identify the authoritative literature indicated by the following citations:
    a. C11.101
    b. P16.147
    c. F80.101

Exercises 11–13 relate to the use of the FASB *Accounting Standards Original Pronouncements.*

11. What paragraphs of the original APB Opinion No. 11 have been superseded?

12. Referring to FASB Statement No. 5, "Accounting for Contingencies," identify the paragraph numbers for the following components of the Statement.
    a. Introduction
    b. Standard of accounting and reporting
    c. Effective date
    d. Examples or illustrations
    e. Background
    f. Basis for standard

13. Referring to APB Opinion No. 26, "Early Extinguishment of Debt," identify the paragraph numbers for the following components of the Opinion.
    a. Introduction
    b. Background
    c. Opinion
    d. Effective date
    e. Examples of illustrations

C H A P T E R 6

OTHER RESEARCH TOOLS

Learning Objectives

After completing this chapter, you should understand:

- How the AICPA's *Accounting Trends and Techniques, Financial Report Surveys,* and *Audit and Accounting Manual* can assist the research effort.

- What is contained in the public files of the accounting and auditing authoritative bodies.

- The major trade directories, government publications, statistical sources, and business and international services available to the researcher.

- The characteristics of the major accounting and auditing computerized research tools that are currently available.

- The importance of the Internet as a research tool.

- The basic techniques of "how to" utilize the Internet for accounting and auditing research.

The previous chapters have presented practical guidance for conducting accounting and auditing research. Chapter 5 dealt with the search for authoritative support through the use of traditional manual research tools—the FASB's
Accounting Standards and the AICPA's *Index to Accounting and Auditing Technical Pronouncements, Professional Standards,* and *Technical Practice Aids.*
This chapter focuses on other manual research tools, but will emphasize computerized research tools currently available to the researcher.

Due to the increase in accounting and attestation pronouncements and the
increase in financial reporting in general, more and more organizations are utilizing computerized research tools to gain rapid access to key information for
decision making. Of major importance for the accounting professional is the
use of the Internet—the "Information Superhighway." A significant section of
this chapter will address the issues of what the Internet is and how it is accessed
and utilized for accounting and auditing research. Also, it should be noted that
a second disk enclosed with this text is a user's guide to utilizing the Internet.
This electronic text is provided free with permission from the Electronic Frontier Foundation in Washington, D.C. More on the use of this disk will be discussed later in this chapter.

Manual Research Tools

In addition to those discussed in Chapter 5, other frequently used manual
research tools include the *Accounting and Tax Index;* the AICPA's *Accounting Trends and Techniques, Financial Report Surveys,* and *Audit and Accounting
Manual;* research files of public accounting firms; and public files of the
accounting and auditing authoritative bodies.

Accounting & Tax Index. The *Accounting & Tax Index* is based in part
on the former *Accountants' Index,* which was published by the AICPA ending
in 1991. This new index, published by UMI, is a comprehensive subject/author
index. The index, which is arranged in a dictionary format with full citations,
covers virtually every English-language publication on accounting or account-
ing-related subjects, such as accounting and tax, and also incorporates
accounting firms, policies and standards, state and national legislation, compensation plans, consulting services, and corporate financial management. The
index, published in three quarterly issues and a cumulative year-end volume,
provides quick access to a number of books, articles, pamphlets, speeches, and
government documents. Figure 6-1 presents an excerpt from the index.

Accounting Trends & Techniques. The AICPA currently publishes
an annual survey of accounting practices entitled *Accounting Trends &
Techniques.* This publication provides a comprehensive up-to-date coverage of

FIGURE 6-1   Excerpts from *Accounting & Tax Index*

EXPENSE ACCOUNTS

Above the line. *Forbes*, v153n4, Feb 14, 1994 - p. 82.

Firm focus: Establishing guidelines and limits, by Anita Dennis. *Journal of Accountancy*, v176n6, Dec 1993 - p. 85.

Fraud findings: Review of executive travel expanses? Why bother? by Courtenay Thompson. *Internal Auditor*, v51n4, Aug 1994 - p. 70-71.

How companies serve up savings, by Fiona Gibb. *Sales & Marketing Management*, v146n10, Sep 1994 - p. 52.

The rapid-refund expense report. *Inc.*, v16n9, Sep 1994 - p. 95–97.

Suite good-byes: Tax tips for today's business travelers by Shelly Branch. *Money*, v23n6, Jun 1994 - p. 137–139.

Travel tip: Getting the most from a hotel, by Anita Dennis. *Journal of Accountancy*, v176n6, Dec 1993 - p. 85–86.

EXPENSE REDUCTION ANALYSTS

Save and prosper, by Sarah Perrin. *Accountancy Age*, AA Magazine, May 1994 - p. 31–34.

EXPERIENCE

Accounting Education Change Commission - Improving the Early Employment Experience of Accountants: Issues Statement No. 4. *Issues in Accounting Education*, v8n2, Fall 1993 - p. 431–435.

After the exams, where next? by Chris Hermannsen. *Management Accounting-London*, v72n9, Oct 1994 - p. 59.

Auditor attendance to negative and positive information: The effect of experience-related differences, by Brenda H. Anderson, Mario Maletta. *Behavioral Research in Accounting*, v6, 1994 - p. 1–20.

CFPs can win PFS designation by substituting experience for testing.

Bowman's Accounting Report, v8n10, Oct 1994 - p. 8.

CFPs case exam eligibility to lure more CPAs. *Accounting Today*, v8n3, Feb 7, 1994 - p. 2.

A cognitive characterization of audit analytical review; Discussion, by Lisa Koonce, Norman R. Walker, et al. *Auditing: A Journal of Practice & Theory*, v12 (Audit Judgment Symposium Supplement), 1993 - p. 57–81.

CPAs must stand up and be counted, by Andrew B. Blackman. *Financial Planning*, v23n1, Jan 1994 - p. 108–111.

The effect of experience on consensus of going-concern judgments, by Joanna L. Ho. *Behavioral Research in Accounting*, v6, 1994 - p. 160–177.

Identification of auditors' propositions related to assessments of management estimates, by George F. Klersey. *Behavioral Research in Accounting*, v6, 1994 - p. 43–71.

Potential adverse effects of specialization within accounting firms, by James P. Angelini, Marguerite R. Hutton, et al. *Accounting Horizons*, v8n3, Sep 1994 - p. 36–47.

The impact of control policies on the process and outcomes of negotiated transfer pricing, by Penelope Sue Greenberg, Ralph H. Greenberg, et al. *Journal of Management Accounting Research*, v6, Fall 1994 - p. 93–127.

Privileged traders and asset market efficiency: A laboratory study, by Daniel Friedman, *Journal of Financial & Quantitative Analysis*, v28n4, Dec 1993 - p. 515–534.

SR & ED tax credits: Are you getting yours? (Part 1), by Glen M. Schmidt. *CGA Magazine*, v28n6, June 1994 - p. 34–37+.

FIGURE 6-1 (continued)

EXPERT SYSTEMS
see also Artificial intelligence; Software packages

Accounting expert systems, by L. Craig Foltin, L. Murphy Smith. *CPA Journal,* v64n11, Nov 1994 - p. 46–53.

Artificial ingredients, by Sara Hedberg. *CIO,* v7n16, Jun 1, 1994 - p. 72–79.

Auditors' knowledge organization: Observations from audit practice and their implications, by Jean C. Bedard, Lynford E. Graham Jr. *Auditing: A Journal of Practice & Theory,* v13n1, Spring 1994 - p. 73–83.

Automated disaster recovery plan auditing: Prospects for using expert systems to evaluate disaster recovery plans, by Albert Marcella Jr, James Rauff. *Edpacs: The EDP Audit, Control, & Security Newsletter,* v21n9, Mar 1994 - p. 1–16.

Automated dynamic audit programme tailoring: An expert system approach: Discussion, by Peter Gillett, Miklos A. Vasarhelyi. *Auditing: A Journal of Practice & Theory,* v12 (Audit Judgment Symposium Supplement), 1993 - p. 173–193.

CCH debuts knowledge-based tax software line. *Accounting Today,* v8n8, May 2, 1994 - p. 23.

CCH's newest tax resource, by Laurence K. Zuckerman, *Accounting Technology,* v10n7, Aug 1994 - p. 58–60.

Expert controllers? *Controllers Update,* n116, Aug 1994 - p. 2–4.

Expert systems and the accounting standard setting process (*111.1C), by Jane Culvenor. *Working Paper (University of New England, Armidale, NSW),* no. 93-1, Aug 1993 - p. 1–19.

Expert systems for minimum scope estimating in the process industries, by Robert L. Steinberger. *American Association of Cost Engineers Transactions,* 1994 Transactions, 1994 - p. SI4.1–SI4.9.

Expert Systems in Business and Finance: Issues and Applications, reviewed by Eric L. Denna. *Accounting Review,* v69n2, Apr 1994 - p. 422–423.

The fast lane to success with NAFTA, by Bob Armstrong, Jeff Patterson. *CA Magazine,* v127n8, Oct 1994 - p. 49–51.

The future of expert systems, by L. Craig Foltin. *National Public Accountant,* v39n7, Jul 1994 - p. 28–31+.

Source: Reprinted with permission from *UMI, copyrighted, 1994.*

---

financial reporting practices and developments, illustrating the current reporting practices of a selected group of companies and charting significant trends in reporting practices. The companies surveyed are all publicly held, and 90 percent of them are listed on the New York or American Stock Exchanges.

The survey enables the practitioner to determine how various size companies in a wide range of industries have complied with the professional standards as they relate to financial reporting. It also alerts the practitioner to emerging trends in reporting practices. Specific reporting requirements set forth in pronouncements of the APB, FASB, and SEC are cited wherever applicable.

Each company surveyed in *Accounting Trends & Techniques* is assigned a reference number. As companies are removed from the survey because of acquisition or merger, the identification number is retired. There is an appendix listing the companies in the order of their reference number. The survey contains a table of contents listing specific reporting and disclosure examples by the general categories of Balance Sheet, Income Statement, Stockholders Equity, Statement of Cash Flows, and Auditor's Report. A topical index is included at the end of the survey. An excerpt from *Accounting Trends & Techniques* is illustrated in Figure 6-2.

Financial Report Surveys. The AICPA's *Financial Report Surveys,* intended to supplement the overview provided by *Accounting Trends and Techniques,* are a continuing series of studies designed to show in detail how specific accounting and reporting questions are actually being handled in the financial reports of companies in a wide range of industries. The surveys include numerous illustrations drawn from the National Automated Accounting Research System (NAARS), which stores data collected from thousands of published financial reports. NAARS is explained later in this chapter. The surveys also include the complete texts of official pronouncements and other pertinent material wherever applicable. To date, the AICPA has published 46 surveys, each focusing in depth on a specific issue of financial reporting.

Audit and Accounting Manual. The *Audit and Accounting Manual,* prepared by the staff of the AICPA, provides a nonauthoritative guide for practitioners in the conduct of an audit. The manual explains and illustrates the actual procedures involved in major aspects of an audit engagement. Extensive examples of such items as engagement letters, audit programs, working papers, and various other forms and documents are provided. The contents of the manual include the following:

- Introduction
- Compilation and Review
- Engagement Planning and Administration
- Internal Control Structure
- Audit Approach and Programs
- Working Papers
- Correspondence, Confirmations, and Representations
- Audit Risk Alerts
- Supervision, Review, and Report Processing
- Accountants' Reports
- Quality Control Forms and Aids

Examples and exhibits in the manual are presented for illustrative purposes only. Many sections, however, provide references to authoritative

FIGURE 6-2 Excerpt from *Accounting Trends & Techniques*

ALLOWANCE FOR DOUBTFUL ACCOUNTS

Table 2-7 summarizes the captions used by the survey companies to describe an allowance for doubtful accounts. *APB Opinion No. 12* states that such allowances should be deducted from the related receivables and appropriately disclosed.

TABLE 2-7: DOUBTFUL ACCOUNT CAPTIONS

	1993	1992	1991	1990
Allowance for doubtful accounts	266	265	273	269
Allowance	164	156	157	150
Allowance for losses	28	28	24	23
Allowance for uncollectible accounts ...	10	9	9	11
Reserve	13	11	14	13
Reserve for doubtful accounts	5	6	6	7
Other caption titles....	33	29	26	24
	519	504	509	497
Receivables shown net	15	14	12	19
No reference to doubtful accounts	66	82	79	84
Total companies	**600**	**600**	**600**	**600**

INVENTORIES

Chapter 4 of *Accounting Research Bulletin No. 43* states that the "primary basis of accounting for inventories is cost . . ." but "a departure from the cost basis of pricing the inventory is required when the utility of the goods is no longer as great as its cost . . ." Approximately 90% of the survey companies use lower of cost or market, an acceptable basis for pricing inventories when circumstances require a departure from cost, to price all or a portion of their inventories.

Table 2-8 summarizes the methods used by the survey companies to determine inventory costs and indicates the portion of inventory cost determined by LIFO. As indicated in Table 2-8, it is not uncommon for a company to use more than one method in determining the total cost of inventory. Methods of inventory cost determination classified as Other in Table 2-8 include specific identification, accumulated costs for contracts in process, and "current cost."

Fifty-eight companies disclosed that certain LIFO inventory levels were reduced with the result that net income was increased due to the matching of older historical cost with present sales dollars. Twenty-three companies disclosed the effect on income from using LIFO rather than FIFO or average cost to determine inventory cost.

Table 2-9 shows by industry classification the number of companies using LIFO and the percentage relationship of those companies using LIFO to the total number of companies in a particular industry classification.

Examples of disclosure and reporting practices for inventories follow.

FIFO

TRANSTECHNOLOGY CORPORATION (MAR)

	1993	1992
Current assets:		
Cash and cash equivalents	$1,505,000	$ 798,000
Accounts receivable:		
United States Government	2,075,000	4,090,00
Commercial (net of allowance for doubtful accounts of $318,000 in 1993 and $268,000 in 1992)	17,426,000	16,314,000
Income tax receivable	59,000	1,123,000
Inventories	33,375,000	32,407,000
Prepaid expenses and other current assets	1,656,000	5,674,000
Deferred income taxes	3,393,000	4,514,000
Net assets of discontinued businesses	3,176,000	8,881,000
Total current assets	62,665,000	73,801,000

FIGURE 6-2 Excerpt from *Accounting Trends & Techniques (continued)*

NOTES TO CONSOLIDATED FINAN-CIAL STATEMENTS

1 (in Part): Summary of Accounting Principles

Inventories

Inventories are stated at the lower of cost or market. Cost is determined by using the first-in, first-out method. Cost includes material, labor and manufacturing overhead costs.

3. Inventories

Inventories at March 31, 1993 and 1992 are summarized as follows:

	1993	1992
Finished goods	$ 4,913,000	$4,753,000
Work-in-process:		
U.S. Government contracts	1,412,000	1,414,000
Commercial	5,412,000	7,192,000
Purchased and manufactured parts	21,638,000	19,648,000
	33,375,000	33,007,000
Less: Progress payments on U.S. government contracts	—	(600,000)
Total	$33,375,000	$32,407,000

TABLE 2-8: INVENTORY COST DETERMINATION

	Number of Companies			
	1993	1992	1991	1990
Methods				
First-in first-out (fifo)	417	415	421	411
Last-in first-out (lifo)	348	358	361	366
Average cost	189	193	200	195
Other	42	45	50	44
Use of LIFO				
All inventories	17	23	23	20
50% or more of inventories	191	189	186	186
Less than 50% of inventories	91	91	95	92
Not determinable	49	55	57	68
Companies using LIFO	**348**	**358**	**361**	**366**

Source: Reprinted with permission granted from American Institute of CPAs, Copyright 1994.

pronouncements in the AICPA *Professional Standards*. The *Audit and Accounting Manual* is available in an annual paperback edition or as a looseleaf subscription service.

Research Files of Public Accounting Firms.

Many public accounting firms maintain research files on various accounting and auditing issues documented from the firm's own practice. The primary purpose of such a file is to provide firm personnel with access to previously researched issues and the firm's conclusions. The research file's design can be as simple or advanced as necessary to meet the firm's needs.

When confronted with a research issue, the practitioner searches the file index to determine if the issue has been previously researched and, if so, where the details of the research can be located. The index is typically an alphanumeric listing by subject matter of topics that are stored in the research files. The details of the research are often stored on computer diskettes to reduce storage costs.

FASB, AcSEC, EITF, and ASB Files. The public files of the FASB, AcSEC, EITF, and ASB contain useful information for the researcher. The public files include all exposure drafts, letters of comment in response to the drafts, minutes of meetings, agenda items, and other correspondence related to the development of professional standards and other pronouncements, such as interpretations. The information contained in these files provides valuable insight in determining the rationale of the various boards or committees in developing standards.

General Business Research Tools

Some of the major business research tools that are available to the researcher in gathering business or statistical information include the following:

Trade Directories.   If one is researching information about an individual business and/or the products it makes, buys, or sells, a trade directory might be useful. There are a number of comprehensive directories that are indispensable in general business research. The main directories include *The Million Dollar Directory,* which provides a listing of U.S. companies; *Thomas Register of American Manufacturers;* and *America's Corporate Families* and *Who Owns Whom,* which provide information on linkages between parent companies and their subsidiaries.

Government Publications.   The U.S. Government is the world's largest publisher. In addition to U.S. Government publications, many state and local governments publish information useful in business research. A sample of the major publications include *Census of Retail Trade, Census of Manufacturers, Census of Services Industries, Census of Transportations, Survey of Current Business,* and the *Federal Reserve Bulletin.*

Statistical Sources.   In order to aid the researcher in the collection of statistical information, the U.S. Government developed a classification system called the Standard Industrial Classification Code (SIC). This system consists of a four-digit code for all manufacturers and nonmanufacturing industries. Some of the major statistical sources that utilize this SIC code system are the *Handbook of Basic Economic Statistics,* the *Statistical Abstract of the United States,* and *Standard and Poor's Statistical Service.*

Business Services.   Many private organizations provide business services that supply summarized financial information on all major American companies. *Moody's Investors Service,* one of the better known services, publishes a weekly *Manual* in each of six business areas: transportation, industrials, OTC (over-the-counter) industrials, public relations, banks and finance, and municipals and governments.   Other business services include *Corporate Records,* published by Standard and Poor's Corporation, along with their services *Value Line* and *Investment Service.*

International Services.   Information for the international business researcher is available in a number of documents. *Principal International Businesses* lists basic information on major companies located around the world. For statistical information, one can use such services as the *Index to International Statistics, Statistical Yearbook,* or *Worldcasts.*

Computerized Research Tools

Computerized document retrieval systems are now a commercial reality. They are used extensively in the medical and legal professions and have gained wide acceptance in the accounting profession. Such retrieval systems enable the researcher to search quickly through large masses of data for those words that are pertinent to his or her inquiry, which in turn make reference to authoritative pronouncements or other topical sources of information. The retrieval system is a computerized system designed to retrieve from a vast library or collection of data (database) those documents that contain a specified pattern of words, phrases, numbers, or combination of these that are likely to occur in accounting materials. The specified pattern is formulated by the researcher as a document search request. In formulating the search request, the researcher attempts to select a pattern of words that will result in a listing of all documents in the database that contain that pattern. The apparent useful features of such a retrieval system are the readily accessible location of the research materials as well as the time savings when compared to a manual search. Examples of the basic applications of these databases by accountants or auditors include the following:

- Using analytical procedures to compare a client to other companies in its industry.
- Obtaining a more in-depth understanding of current developments in the client's industry.

- Obtaining timely notice to any pending changes to the tax laws, forms, or regulations.
- Inquiring into executive backgrounds of new potential clients.

However, the practitioner faces the basic risk of missing an authoritative document or other piece of information if the document does not contain the exact word pattern called for in the document search request. Careful selection of word patterns is important; therefore, the researcher might need either to expand in some cases or reduce the word selection pattern in the search for specific information on a particular database. The remaining portion of this chapter, therefore, will highlight the capabilities of the major computerized retrieval systems as well as the research tasks that can be carried out with each database. Following is a summary of these databases.

National Automated Accounting Research System.
NAARS, an acronym for National Automated Accounting Research System, is a computerized information retrieval system developed by the AICPA and Mead Data Central, Inc. (MDC). This research system has revolutionized the research function that supports the accounting profession and is the primary research system currently being utilized by accountants. Through the use of a terminal linked to MDC's computer system, a researcher is able to access the financial statements, footnotes, and auditors' reports of over 20,000 listed and over-the-counter companies, selected proxy statement information, and all authoritative pronouncements, both current and superseded, of the AICPA, FASB, and SEC that relate to financial reporting. This database provides one with up-to-date as well as immediate information in order to locate the issues and answers to present day practical problems.

Presently, the NAARS library consists of the following active files:

Annual Report File—This file includes reports of corporations whose stock is traded on the New York or American Stock Exchanges, or those companies traded over-the-counter. Information included consists of financial statements; *Fortune* rankings; auditors' reports; balance sheet data, including current assets, equity, and net income; interim data; and foreign currency exchange gains and losses.

Literature File—All current as well as superseded authoritative and semi-authoritative accounting literature is readily available through NAARS. Information included in this file contains the SEC regulations and accounting releases; Statements and Interpretations of the FASB, CASB, GASB, and the International Accounting Standards Committee; APB Opinions; and Accounting Research Bulletins and the Statements on Auditing Standards.

Proxy File—This file contains selected information from proxy statements of *Fortune*-ranked companies. This information includes non-audit accounting fees, legal proceedings and related-party transactions, and corporate board structure.

NAARS has the following characteristics that make it a unique retrieval system. First, it is a "full-text" system rather than a system that simply provides abstracts of documents. The system provides a comprehensive version of documents that are stored in the computer and readily displayed for review. Each word of every document on file is recorded in the database and each word of the text is treated as an index term. Therefore, the researcher can retrieve a document based upon the words in the document. The research display could include the full text of the document, a specific segment, or a search word surrounded by a small amount of the text in order to determine the context of the search word. Thus, the system is considered a "free text" searchable system.

Second, NAARS is a real-time system whereby the researcher, using a terminal or a portable computer (PC), can communicate directly with the database via telephone lines from the researcher's office. Costly delays are greatly reduced through this direct communication with the computer.

Third, the system operates in an interactive mode, which permits the researcher to carry on a dialogue with the computer, providing the opportunity to broaden or narrow the research to retrieve precisely the information needed.

Finally, the availability of the system allows access 23 hours a day Monday–Friday and $14\frac{1}{2}$ hours a day on Saturday, Sunday, and holidays.

Typical applications of the NAARS system would include answers to the following types of questions or issues:

- What are consolidation policies for subsidiaries that are less than 100 percent owned?
- Balance sheet presentation of unfunded pension liabilities.
- Which CPA firm audited which companies?
- Examples of double-dated audit reports.
- *Fortune* 500 ranking of a company.
- Disclosure of pending government investigations.
- Footnote disclosure requirements for leases.

With such a comprehensive search, the researcher can have more confidence that a thorough search has taken place, and if no authoritative pronouncement is identified, the accountant might turn to the conceptual framework project of the FASB to develop a solution or to other firms' approaches as precedents.

LEXIS/NEXIS.   The LEXIS/NEXIS library, a large set of databases, is a service of Mead Data Central consisting of the full text of all articles carried in approximately 200 newspapers, magazines, and wire services including the

New York Times, American Banker, Dun's Review, U.S. News and World Report, Washington Post, P.R. Newswire, as well as other publications and wire services. The following types of searches illustrate how this database could be utilized:

- To locate earnings reports for a particular company. Various publications contained in this library regularly report the earnings of many public companies.
- To locate background information on the president of a new client or the company itself.
- To monitor an issue with international dimensions that have a direct impact on your client, such as the Mideast oil cartel and the resulting impact on oil prices.
- To determine which public companies have recently gone through reorganization.

ABI/INFORM.   This system contains citations with abstracts to articles appearing in approximately 1,400 international periodicals covering business and management topics and related functional areas such as accounting and auditing.

Disclosure.   Disclosure, Incorporated, offers a number of software packages and databases for commercial use. Specific details of these products and discussion of the student version included with this text are presented in Chapter 7.

In addition to the primary databases previously highlighted, other databases available with features appropriate for accounting and auditing research are briefly described below.

DIALOG.   DIALOG, prepared by DIALOG Information Services, Inc., is an online service that incorporates the full-text or abstracts of many journal articles relating to accounting and tax issues. The service provides databases that extract information on a variety of subjects. Such topics include agriculture, energy, business, economics, governmental publications, chemistry, law, medicine, science, and engineering. Also available on DIALOG is PREDICASTS, which provides extensive industry information including market data, product design, resource use, and technology information. Another DIALOG database is the Marquis Who's Who file, which contains detailed biographies of thousands of top professionals. This file would be useful to the auditor in the investigation of management of a potential new audit client.

Standard & Poor's Database Services.   These computerized databases contain information from Standard & Poor's *Corporation Descriptions,*

Corporate First Facts, and the *Daily News.* Up-to-date information in the databases include interim earnings, dividends, contract awards, management changes, bond descriptions, and mergers, all available through DIALOG.

BNA.   The Bureau of National Affairs, Inc. (BNA) provides a number of databases of importance for the accounting and auditing researcher. The major databases include:

- BNA Antitrust & Trade Regulation Daily
- BNA Bankruptcy Law Daily
- BNA Daily News from Washington
- BNA Environmental Law
- BNA Financial Service
- BNA International Business & Finance Daily

Information Access Company Online Databases.   Information

Access Company is one of the world's leading suppliers of periodical indexes. Founded and staffed by professional librarians and information specialists, Information Access Company provides access to over 3 million articles from over 2,500 journals, tabloids, newsletters, and newspapers. Major databases of value to the accounting/auditing researcher include the following, which are also available through the DIALOG service.

1. **Magazine Index.** A general research tool that covers current affairs, business, education, consumer information, home and leisure activities, performing arts, science, and travel.
2. **Trade and Industry Index.** An invaluable source of information on business and technological developments for all major industries. The Index provides information on new products, company mergers, personnel, management, technological innovations, the regulatory environment, industry trends, forecasts, and statistics.
3. **National Newspaper Index.** A leading source for news from five of the most important nationally distributed newspapers. Business information includes contracts, mergers, products, companies, current affairs, people, social conditions, scientific developments, and consumer issues.
4. **Annual Report Abstracts.** This database contains more than 250,000 records of annual report summaries for publicly held U.S. corporations and selected international companies whose securities are traded on U.S. stock exchanges.
5. **Management Contents.** Current information provided by Management Contents includes a wide variety of business and management topics. Researchers will find pertinent information on marketing, accounting, organizational behavior, public administration, and more.

AICPA's Electronic Body of Knowledge

In order to enhance the research process in the review of the volumes of authoritative literature that exists, the AICPA has developed a series of its publications in electronic format. To date, the AICPA has developed its Integrated Practice System (IPS), a package containing the AICPA's successful software, a series of engagement manuals, and various training materials, all in electronic format. The AICPA has provided the following publications, previously explained, on diskettes as part of their IPS package:

- **Electronic Index to Technical Publications**—an electronic formatting of the *Index to Accounting & Auditing Technical Pronouncements.*

- **Professional Standards - Volume 1**—the electronic formatting of the *Codification of Statements on Auditing Standards and Standards for Attestation Engagements.*

- **Professional Standards - Volume 2**—the entire contents of the manual version of *Professional Standards - Volume 2* on computer disk.

- **Audit and Accounting Guides**—the electronic version of the indispensable Audit and Accounting Guide Loose-leaf Subscription Service.

- **Technical Practice Aids**—the electronic version of the nonauthoritative response to inquiries received by the experts at the AICPA's Technical Information Service.

In addition to the above-named research tools, the AICPA currently provides other electronically formatted publications and software as computerized aids for the practitioner. The AICPA has also established an online service for members called the "Accountants' Forum." This service will allow members to have electronic access to the Institute's professional literature, exposure drafts, legislative alerts, newsletters, and other information sources. Through the forum, members will be able to communicate with each other on the forum's bulletin boards and e-mail system.

Accounting and Auditing Research via the Internet

The Internet is a tool that will have a significant impact on the way accounting students and professionals will do business and, in particular, accounting and auditing research. The Internet, often referred to as the information superhighway, is a global resource that connects millions of users through intercommunicating networks. Such a resource permits the researcher to accomplish the following major tasks:

- Send and receive electronic mail. *E-mail* is the term that describes the transmitting of a message from one user to another by using an electronic network. E-mail is generally text data. However, more and more e-mail includes graphic images and binary files. In the near future, it will not be uncommon for e-mail to include audio and video data. Currently, auditors use e-mail to communicate with other auditors to request assistance in audit planning, share audit techniques, or even transfer audit programs.
- Discuss various accounting or auditing issues by participating in discussion groups. Figure 6-3 presents a sample of discussion groups on Anet, a joint venture between Australian and American academics that provides Internet services to accountants around the world. Accountants have used newsgroups to confer with fellow experts to obtain answers to technical questions. Currently, various industry groups are also beginning to establish a presence on the Internet. Even CPA firms, both large and small, are providing information concerning their firms via the Internet.
- Search for accounting or auditing information. Accountants have used the Internet to search for legislation, either federal or state, that may have an impact on clients. Another major use of the Internet is the retrieval of financial statements from SEC filings through the SEC's EDGAR (Electronic Data Gathering and Retrieval System).

FIGURE 6-3   Sample of Anet Discussion Groups

Mailing List Name	Purpose
AAccSys-L	Provides discussion concerning matters on accounting information systems theory and practice.
AAudit-L	Provides discussion on issues related to external and internal auditing.
AEthics-L	Provides discussion on the ethical dimensions of accounting and auditing.
AFinAcc-L	Provides discussion dealing with issues of financial accounting.
AIntSysL	Provides discussion relating to the application of artificial intelligence and expert systems in accounting.
ATaxL	Provides discussion on all aspects of tax accounting.

Figure 6-4 is just one example of how the Internet can help a small CPA firm provide practical services to clients. From the example, one can conclude that the Internet is changing society on a worldwide basis. Now is the time to become familiar with the Internet in order to be prepared for the 21st century. The following sections will aid you in becoming more proficient with this exciting and dynamic research tool. You will be astounded by the data that is available on the Internet.

The Internet.   The Internet can be thought of as a spiderweb of thousands of communication networks that physically cover the globe. It began in 1969 in the U.S. Department of Defense under the acronym ARPANET (Advanced Research Project Agency Network). Its purpose was to make military networks less tolerant to failure by providing many paths between computers. This design made the system more reliable in that the computers connected to the system could send messages by any path. Therefore, if one part of the system failed, the other computers would redirect the message by another route, resulting in no lost connection or data. Throughout the past 20 years, additional networks were added to ARPANET and the system has grown to its present size with various acronym changes to the current name "Internet." This system is utilized by millions of users daily around the world.

Navigating the Internet.   A major challenge after accessing the Internet is the attempt to understand where and how to search for information. The major techniques for accessing data and searching ("surfing") on the Internet are briefly presented below. Each of these techniques will be further explained as you utilize the enclosed disk that accompanies this text. This disk contains a guide to the Internet, which is provided free to you with permission from the Electronic Frontier Foundation in Washington, D.C. By utilizing this disk and following the interactive tutorial presented later in this section, you will complete a basic course on "how to" navigate the Internet.

FTP.   File Transfer Protocol (FTP) is a method of moving files from one computer to another. By using a standard protocol system, file transfers can take place regardless of the type of computer one is using for file transfers.

Vast libraries of files exist on the thousands of systems connected to the Internet. One can obtain free or low-cost shareware programs to copies of various documents, such as recent corporate filings with the SEC or a recent Supreme Court decision. The basic way of obtaining these files is through the use of the file transfer protocol system.

However, in order to find the file you want to transfer, which can be quite time consuming, a database system was created that automatically and on a regular basis searches the Internet and indexes files into a single searchable

---

FIGURE 6-4   An Example of a Small CPA Firm Utilizing the Internet

Mark Jensen, CPA, states that the Internet has become the "greatest equalizer" because it provides his small practice with many of the research tools utilized by the Big Six accounting firms. "It lets me offer resources and services to my clients and future clients that the big firms have to offer," says Jensen.

Mark was asked by a would-be entrepreneur to help write a business plan to open a computer software store in southern New York. Both Jensen and the client were computer literate, but neither of them knew much about the software business. So, Mark accessed the Internet and within an hour was deluged with information about software stores.

A word search for "software" yielded more than 100 articles about computer stores, including one from the *Washington Post* about a software store start-up. Jensen also gleaned information about software stores from the small business forums on the Internet. Mark and his client used the information to prepare a business plan that helped secure financing for the business.

Being online via the Internet allows Jensen to search through news sources throughout the world. Publications and news services such as the *New York Times*, Associated Press, United Press International, Reuters, *Financial Times of London*, and the Dow Jones News Service are just a few of the sources available on the Internet.

Mark also retrieves news items for clients as an effective way to maintain relationships and attract new clients. One of his clients is involved in the machine tools industry and he frequently notifies the client when a major industry event takes place.

Besides tracking news, Jensen uses the Internet to exchange e-mail with clients and associates. He also can access the SEC's Edgar System and obtain recent SEC filings of major public companies such as their 10-K, 10-Q, or other filings.

---

database called "Archie." Therefore, one accesses this database (Archie) and searches the index of files for the particular file needed.

USENET. On the Internet, news and opinions about the state of the world are freely disbursed. Currently, USENET consists of a collection of over 10,000 bulletin-board type discussion groups called newsgroups. All types of news appear on the Internet and USENET is the tool used to access this information. The basic benefit of participating in a newsgroup is that you share ideas with others who have the same interests on a particular subject. These discussions of similar topics resulted in the creation of thousands of newsgroups on the

Internet. A sample of accounting newsgroups was presented in Figure 6-3. A more comprehensive list of accounting and auditing newsgroups in presented in Appendix A.

Gopher. Another tool that makes it easier to search the Internet is Gopher, a client/server system that can be used on a variety of computers. This system, developed by the University of Minnesota—thus its name Gopher—is a menu-type system that organizes computer files by categories and subcategories.

This software system takes a request from a menu selection and then scans the Internet for information. With Gopher, you tunnel through the Internet by the way of various levels of menus as it searches for your requested information. This tool has become very popular for navigating the Internet.

World Wide Web (WWW). Although Gopher is a very popular way for browsing the Internet, it has its limitations. Gopher is structured in a hierarchical menu format. Each menu item leads to other menu items or to a service. However, WWW's structure is where all the Internet's data is considered hypertext. By selecting a keyword in a document, WWW moves you to another document containing that keyword. This document could be on the same computer or a different computer in a foreign country. Having these links (keywords) allows one to search documents interactively rather than just in a linear method.

Two of the most popular browsing tools in the WWW setting are Mosaic and Netscape. These multimedia browsers can not only display documents but also any embedded graphics, video, or sound. These tools have become so popular that some claim they are causing a minor traffic jam on the Internet because their ease of use makes browsing related subjects quick and convenient. Each of these techniques for navigating the Internet will be explained with hands-on exercises as you complete the Internet tutorial that follows.

Tutorial for Navigating the Internet.
To become proficient on the Internet you should complete the following tutorial. Information on your Internet disk that accompanies this text will be required reading material. You can view the text, entitled *EFF's Guide to the Internet,* on your computer, or you can print out the text to read in hard copy format. Whichever you do, you must first load the ASCII file, approximately 200 pages, into your word processor. As you proceed through this tutorial, you will be given certain reading assignments as well as basic exercises to complete on the Internet. HAPPY SURFING THE INTERNET!!

This tutorial provides a number of hands-on lessons to help you become proficient in accessing the Internet. Once you have a working knowledge of this information superhighway, the data available to you as an accounting or auditing researcher will seem unlimited.

Lesson 1. Determine whether your organization (i.e., university or corporation) has access to the Internet. This is a must in order to complete the hands-on exercises. If you do not have access to the Internet, you can still complete the reading assignments in order to gain a better understanding of the Internet.

Ask your organization's Internet administrator how to connect to the Internet and whether your system utilizes e-mail, FTP, Gopher, and/or WWW.

Lesson 2. Read Chapters 1 and 2 of the Internet guide, which explain the procedures of setting up and jacking into the Internet. Chapter 2 explains the basics of using e-mail.

If you do not have access through your university or company's system, which public-access provides service to the Internet in your state?

Electronic messages may be sent and received using many different programs. Some of the most common are Elm, Pine, and Eudora. In order to use electronic mail, you need only have access to the Internet, an e-mail program, and the e-mail address of the person or persons you wish to reach. It's pretty easy. Send an e-mail message to a friend, roommate, or co-worker as described in Chapter 2.

Lesson 3. Read Chapters 3 and 4 of the Internet text. As the text explains, e-mail is normally "one-to-one" discussion, whereas Usenet is "many-to-many." Subscribe to the following newsgroups and browse the discussions taking place.

- Subscribe to the newsgroup: Misc.invest (This resource discusses investments and the handling of money)

- Subscribe to the newsgroup: Rec.sport.golf (This newsgroup discusses all aspects of golf)

Lesson 4. Read Chapter 5 of the Internet text on Mailing Lists and Bitnet. Figure 6-3 and Appendix A in Chapter 6 of the *Accounting and Auditing Research* text present a number of mailing lists about various topics. Select the list name AFinAcc-L from Figure 6-3. What is the topical discussion? Subscribe to it and monitor the messages for a few days.

The basic steps to subscribe to this mailing list are as follows:

Step 1— Using e-mail, send the following message:
          listproc@scu.edu.au
Step 2— When the system asks for a subject, leave it blank.
Step 3— In the body of the message type:
          subscribe AFinAcc-L (your_firstname) (your_lastname)
Step 4— Monitor your e-mail messages.

Select any list name of interest to you in Appendix A, subscribe to it, and monitor its messages for a week.

Lesson 5. Read Chapter 6 of the Internet text on Telnet. This chapter explains how you can log into other computers around the world to take advantage of the public programs and services that are offered.

The SEC has joined the Internet. Telnet to **fedworld.gov** and go to the Regulatory Information Mail. Browse the SEC information that is on the Internet.

Lesson 6. Read Chapter 7 of the Internet text on FTP. As discussed in Chapter 6, FTP (File Transfer Protocol) is a tool for transferring files between computers. However, to find files of interest to you, you might want to use Archie.

FTP to the General Accounting Office (GAO) as explained in the Internet text on interesting FTP sites. Determine what types of reports are available from the GAO.

With FTP, one must know the file location in order to access it. However, if you do not know the file location, Archie is a search program that will aid you in your search. Select a keyword, such as "accounting" or "auditing," and use Archie to find the files on the Internet related to your keyword.

Lesson 7. Read Chapters 8 and 9 on Gophers, WAISs, and the World Wide Web (WWW). These advanced tools make it much easier to use the Internet. Utilize Gopher to access the SEC files that you accessed using Telnet in Lesson 5. If you have access to the WWW, use it to access the SEC files. Notice how much easier it is to access information with this advanced tool than either by FTP or Telnetting.

Lesson 8. You should now have a working understanding of the Internet and the tools to access it. Read Chapters 10–15 at your leisure to learn about the uses of the Internet in education and the business world.

Summary

Many research tools are available to the accountant/auditor in conducting practical research. The major tools can be classified as either manual or computerized retrieval systems. As business information in general expands, and with the availability of massive amounts of information through computerized databases, computerized research aided by the microcomputer has no doubt become the primary research methodology. In addition to these major databases, the use of the Internet will be a must in order to conduct effective and efficient accounting and auditing research. Since information is accessible within seconds, the professional will have more time for the more important role of decision maker.

Discussion Questions

1. Describe the contents of the following manual research tools: *Accounting & Tax Index, Accounting Trends and Techniques, Financial Report Surveys,* and *Audit and Accounting Manual.*

2. What is the purpose of a public accounting firm's research file?

3. List some advantages of computerized document retrieval systems over manual research.

4. What is the basic risk of utilizing a computerized retrieval system?

5. What data files are currently available in the NAARS library?

6. Identify the four major characteristics of NAARS.

7. Identify three possible applications of the NAARS system.

8. What is included in the AICPA's Electronic Body of Knowledge?

9. What is the contents of the LEXIS/NEXIS library?

10. Describe briefly the contents of the following databases: Information Access Company Online, DIALOG, ABI/INFORM, and Standard & Poor's Database Services.

11. What is the Internet? Briefly explain three ways the Internet can be utilized by the professional accountant/auditor.

12. What are the four basic ways of navigating the Internet?

13. Identify three Anet Discussion Groups available to the accountant/auditor.

14. What is the AICPA's "Accountants' Forum"? Suggest two ways that it could be utilized by the practitioner.

APPENDIX A
Kaplan's AuditNet Resource List (ARL)

This Internet resource list is prepared and copyrighted by James M. Kaplan. This list is reproduced here with permission of James M. Kaplan. This list is periodically updated and can be located on the Internet at the following URL:

http://www.unf.edu/misc/mayer/arl.html

This list presents a summary of some the major electronic resources available to accountants and auditors via the Internet and commercial information services. Section A presents new resources or modifications to the Resource List. Section B presents an alphabetical listing of the electronic resources that are available for accounting and auditing research purposes.

Section A—New Resources, Modifications, or Resources No Longer Available

AuditNet Resource List (ARL) New Distribution Points—list of electronic resources available for auditors via Internet mailing lists and commercial information services. Updated on a monthly basis. The ARL is available on the FinanceNet gopher and WWW site. Also available on IGNet at gopher:

//www.sbaonline.sba.gov:70/11/ignet

and the ETSU gopher homepage at gopher:

//etsuodt.etsu.edu:70/11/Administrative%20Departments/Internal%20Audits

> **Please note that a hypertext (html) version of the AuditNet Resource List (ARL) is now available. Those of you who are using the World Wide Web (WWW) may visit the ARL Homepage by pointing your browser to the URL
>
> http://www.unf.edu/misc/jmayer/arl.html

ANet Mailing Lists—ATechno-L will be moderated by Miles Gietzmann in Copenhagen <iqmiles@cbs.dk>. The mailing list will promote and report on the use of accounting techniques for the assessment of technological advancements. Subscribe to list by sending e-mail to LISTPROC@scu.edu.au. In the body of the message type SUBSCRIBE followed by ATechno-L and your real name.

Barefoot Auditor (BFA)—Pathfinder, the company that produced the software auditing program Barefoot Auditor, established a WWW site with FTP facilities for program demos and sharing information about how to use BFA. Includes press releases, an introduction to software auditing technology, and information about other network security review tools. URL is:

http://www.u- net.com/pathfinder

Canadian Open Government Pilot—pilot project on the Internet undertaken by Industry Canada to provide greater access to government through information networks. Provides links to Finance Canada, Ernst & Young Canada, TaxSites, Taxing Times, IRS, and the U.S. Tax Code On-Line via the following URL gopher:

//morrison.revcan.ca/11/Other_Resources

Cellular Telecommunications Industry Association (CTIA) Antifraud Internet Mailbox—The CTIA Fraud Task Force set up a hotline tip box for reporting incidents of cellular phone hacking. CTIA is soliciting information on any type of illegal phone activity. The mailbox is administered by Decision Strategies International (DSI), a Washington, D.C., based investigative consulting firm. Send Task Force messages to cell-fraud.tmn.com or anonymously an205326@anon.penet.fi. Encrypted messages can also be sent using PGP. The PGP public key for Decision Strategies can be obtained by sending an e-mail message to key@four11.com, with dsi@tmn.com in the body of the message.

Columbia University Internal Audit—the URL changed to:

http://www.columbia.edu/cu/ia/

East Texas State University—ETSU established a Gopher HomePage that includes the Audit Resources List, Contingency Planning/Disaster Recovery Planning Guidelines, Information Security Standards, Information Security & Risk Management (Policy, Standards and Guidelines) and more. URL gopher:

//etsuodt.etsu.edu:70/11/Administrative%20Departments/Internal%20Audits

GAO Report Database on the Internet—all General Accounting Office reports are now available on the Internet through the Government Printing Office Access Service. Auditors may telnet to swais.access.gpo.gov and login as GAO. Auditors may dial in to (202) 512-1661 and type SWAIS and then login as GAO. Access via the WWW available soon at the following URL:

http://www.access.gpo.gov

General Accounting Office Reports—GAO high risk, miscellaneous, technical, and transition reports available at:

http:/./www.yahoo.com/Government/Agencies/General_Accounting_Office/

Government Auditing Standards—the GAO Government Auditing Standards or Yellow Book is available at the following URL gopher:

//pula.financenet.gov/00/docs/central/gao/yellow

Government Auditor's Resource Page (GARP)—the U.S. Department of Education Office of Inspector General established a homepage that provides information on resources for government auditors. Includes links to Thomas (legislative information on the Internet), Internet search tools, audit resources, sources for government documents, and links to other government resource indexes. The URL is:

http://www.tmn.com/Community/cbury/GARP.html

The IGNet gopher has moved from the Department of Justice to the Small Business Administration. This change was made to make administration of the gopher more accessible to the IGNet director and executive committee. The new address for the gopher is: <www.sbaonline.sba.gov>. This will put you in the main SBA gopher, which has a menu pick for IGNet. If you want to go directly to the IGNet screen, use the following URL:

<gopher://www.sbaonline.sba.gov:70/11/ignet>

Information Week Interactive—IW is a weekly newsmagazine oriented to business and technology managers. It frequently covers issues of interest to auditors on topics such as security and software management. Good resource for auditors to stay current on information technology hot issues. Provides WAIS search for back issues. The URL is:

http://techweb.cmp.com/iwk

Internet Bulletin for CPAs—For subscription information send e-mail to sales@kentis.kent.oh.us.

Nijenrode Business Resources—comprehensive list of business resources maintained by Nijenrode University in the Netherlands. Provides links to business resources on the Internet. The URL is:

http://www.nijenrode/nl/resources/bus.html

Performance Measurement Info—FinanceNet has a number of files and reports available on performance measurement at gopher:

//pula.financenet.gov:70/11/docs/post/perform

Somar Software—Somar produces Windows NT auditing tools (Somar DumpAcl) which are of interest to computer security auditors. Includes discussion of Windows NT security issues. Somar also has pointers to Windows NT related Web pages, the NIST Computer Security Resource Clearinghouse, and the AuditNet Resource List homepage. The URL is:

http://www.somar.com

Training and Seminar Locator—free access database to help find resources for training and professional development. Search U.S. training providers by type of resource, subject, location, and date range. Eventually, this service will provide on-line registration. The URL is:

http://www.tasl.com/tasl/home.html

Section B—AuditNet Resource List

Accounting, Audit, and Financial Management E-Mail Directory—the AAF e-mail directory is designed to facilitate communication between accounting, audit, and financial management professionals. The directory is maintained by the City of Albuquerque Internal Audit Office and includes financial related mailing lists. The directory includes search by geographic location, industry, or alphabetical. The URL for the directory is:

http://www.cabq.gov/aud/direct.html

ACL mailing list—established March 1, 1995 on America Online to be a moderated ACL discussion forum for the exchange of ideas related to the use of ACL software. ACL is a PC-based software program that allows users to easily read, analyze, and report on data from mainframe, mini, and microcomputers. On a monthly basis, the moderator sends a summarized document that organizes the ideas sent during the previous month. The mailing list is not a forum for technical questions (other than idea questions such as "Is it possible to use ACL for Accounts Receivable testwork and does anyone have a good way to do this?"). All technical assistance questions should be directed to ACL in Vancouver; the phone number is (604) 669-4225. Further assistance and ACL ideas can be located on the ACL Bulletin Board in Vancouver—(604) 669-3277. All messages and subscriptions should be sent to rlanza@aol.com with one line in the body of the letter: SUB ACL. It would be appreciated by the moderator if the person's real name, company, and number of years ACL has been used be included in the message.

ACL Software Users Discussion List—ACL-L is a non-moderated Internet discussion list and forum which is relied on by more than 10,000 users worldwide to exchange ideas and information among authorized users of ACL (Audit Command Language) software. ACL is a PC-based software program which allows users to easily read, analyze, and report on data from mainframe, mini, or microcomputers. Initial subscriptions to the list are screened by the listener to ensure addition of only appropriate individuals. Send subscription request to listserv@etsuadmn.etsu.edu with one line in the body of the letter: SUB ACL-L yourname.

ACUA-L List—Association of College and University Auditors on Bitnet. ACUA-L is a listserve on Bitnet for College and University Auditors. This is a closed list for College and University Auditors. Contact Chuck Jefferis at the University of Vermont (Internet cjefferi@moose.uvm.edu).

Albuquerque, NM Internal Audit Resource Page—the Internal Audit Office of the City of Albuquerque, New Mexico established a World Wide Web page with pointers to useful Internet Resources for auditors. Included are links to Census Data, Code of Federal Regulations, U.S. Code, FinanceNet, and other sources. They also established a comprehensive e-mail directory that includes all audit/accounting/finance related mailing lists as well as e-mail addresses for auditors. This site is an example of how professional internal auditors are finding productive uses for the Internet. The URL for this site is:

http://www.cabq.gov/aud/home.html

American Society for Quality Control (ASQC)—professional organization for persons employed or interested in the field of Quality Science. ASQC maintains a number of files including the AuditNet Resource List. Gopher quality.org, FTP to:

ftp://pub/qc/auditnet

URL is http://www.asqc.org/

URL : (http://www.quality.org/qc

Quality Resources Online—URL is http://www.quality.org/qc

ANet Mailing Lists—Anet is a networked electronic forum in the broad accounting and auditing discipline. Anet mailing lists are also available for the following areas (type subscribe "listname and send to above address): AAUDIT-L (Audit Issues), ANews-L (Accounting/Auditing News), AAccSys-L (Accounting Systems), AEthics-L (Ethics in Accounting and Auditing), AFinAcc-L (Financial Accounting), AIntAcc-L (International Accounting), AMgtAcc-L (Management Accounting), ATeach-L (Accounting Education). Subscribe to list by sending e-mail to LISTPROC@scu.edu.au. In the body of the message, type SUBSCRIBE followed by listname and your real name.

ANet World Wide Web site—ANet maintains a WWW site. The site maintains archives of the 30 Anet mailing lists, a complete list of accounting organizations worldwide, an accounting bibliographic database, and a variety of accounting and auditing resources. An e-mail to anet@scu.edu.au will generate a help file. The ANet WWW site is also mirrored at the Rutgers Accounting Web. URL for the ANet WWW site is:

http://anet.scu.edu.au/anet

Association for Computing Machinery (ACM)—largest and oldest international scientific and educational computer society in the industry. ACM provides members with a forum for sharing knowledge on developments and achievements. There is a Special Interest Group (SIG) for Security, Audit, and Control. The URL is:

http:\\acm.org:80)

Association of Government Accountants (AGA)—The FinanceNet gopher server recently added information on AGA including background, National conference listing, and details of the Certified Government Financial Manager Program, and the DC AGA Newsletter. Also included in the FinanceNet gopher server Government Financial Management Document Libraries is the AGA Report of the Task Force on Performance Auditing. Gopher to financenet.gov to access the AGA documents.

Association of Healthcare Internal Auditors (AHIA)— The only international organization dedicated to the advancement of the healthcare internal auditing profession. AHIA's mission is to promote cost containment, revenue enhancement, and increased productivity in healthcare institutions through internal auditing. AHIA seeks to strengthen healthcare internal auditing by providing for the continuing professional education needs of healthcare internal auditors; providing a forum for sharing information, experience, and ideas; promoting the benefits of healthcare internal auditing to healthcare executives and trustees; and representing the profession to other organizations, government agencies, and the public. While the AHIA does not have a formal e-mail address, further information can be obtained by e-mail to AHIA's Executive Vice President at CharlieDal@aol.com.

Audit-L Discussion List—a generalized audit discussion list open to all auditors regardless of industries and organizations. The list is intended to have a diverse membership so that broad perspectives from all auditors can be gained through interactive communication. While many specialized lists were created to address unique needs of specific industries or special interest groups, the concept of this list recognizes that many audit issues cross industry/organizational lines. Send subscription request to listserv@etsuadmn.etsu.edu with one line in the body of the letter: SUB AUDIT-L yourname.

Auditnet E-mail Listing (AEL)—listing of auditor e-mail addresses for the purpose of fostering electronic communications among audit professionals in government, industry, and academic institutions. Listing in the AEL is by request. Maintained by Jim Kaplan. Send request to Jim Kaplan at one of the listed e-mail addresses and include name, e-mail address, organization name, and areas of interest.

AuditNet Resource List (ARL)—list of electronic resources available for auditors via Internet mailing lists and commercial information services. Updated on a monthly basis and available free of charge. The following are ARL distribution points:

  ANet Auditing List—(AAudit-L@scu.edu.au)

  Australian University Internal Auditors List—
  (IntAudit-L@Levels-UniSa.edu.au)

   CTI Centre—(CTI-ACC-Audit@mailbase.ac.uk)

FinanceNet gopher and WWW site FinanceNet(http:www.financenet.gov)

Internal Audit Usenet Newsgroup(alt.business.internal-audit)

NCSA InfoSecurity Forum (Auditing Files Section) on CIS (GO NCSA). on the FinanceNet gopher and WWW site. Also available on IGNet at gopher:

//www.sbaonline.sba.gov:70/11/ignet

and the ETSU gopher homepage at gopher:

//etsuodt.etsu.edu:70/11/Administrative%20Departments/Internal%20Audits

**Please note that a hypertext (html) version of the AuditNet Resource List (ARL) is now available. Those of you who are using the World Wide Web (WWW) may visit the ARL Homepage by pointing your browser to the URL:

http://www.unf.edu/misc/jmayer/arl.html

To add your listserve or gopher site to this list or for more information e-mail Jim Kaplan at jkaplan@capaccess.org.

Auditor General of Canada—the 1994 Annual Report of the Auditor General of Canada is now available on the Internet. The report contains more than 1,000 pages of detailed information and is organized based on the results of studies and audits completed. Reach the report by gopher access as follows: gopher.phoenix.ca. The URL is gopher:

//gopher.phoenix.ca:70/

Australian Universities Internal Audit Mailing List—Mailing list available to all Internal Audit staff of Australian Universities (and other interested auditors). Send e-mail to the listserve at INTAUDIT-L-REQUEST@Levels.UniSA. Edu.Au and include Subscribe INTAUDIT-L in the subject or message.

Code of Federal Regulations on the WWW—the Code of Federal Regulations is the official subject matter order compilation of Federal regulations of a general applicability and legal effect, that are currently in force. In accordance with section 1510(d) of title 44 of the U.S. Code, the Code of Federal Regulations is compiled by the Office of the Federal Register of the National Archives and Records Administration. The Code is divided into 50 titles by subject matter. Each title is divided into sections. Sections within a title may be grouped together as subtitles, chapters, subchapters, parts, subparts, or divisions. Titles may also have appendices that may be divided into sections, rules, and/or forms. Available from the House of Representatives Internet Library. The URL is:

http://www.pls.com:8001/his/cfr.html

Columbia University Internal Audit—the Columbia University Web site has a section devoted to their Internal Audit Department. The section includes A Guide to Internal Controls, Internal Control Issues, and Auditing at Columbia University: A Service to Management. The last document is an excellent guide that other audit organizations could follow to educate management and departments about internal auditing. The URL for this site is:

http://www.columbia.edu/cu/ia/

Computer Operations, Audit, and Security Technology (COAST) Project— computer security research project in the Computer Science Department at Purdue University. Exploring new approaches to computer security and computer system management. COAST has a comprehensive FTP archive containing nearly 400 mb of tools, papers, technical reports, documentation, announcements, alerts, security patches, and newsletters. Areas of interest include, but are not limited to, access control, authentication, criminal investigation, e-mail privacy, firewalls, and incident response. To access via ftp the URL is:

ftp://coast.cs.purdue.edu/pub

Gopher access via gopher:

//coast.cs.purdue.edu/1/.gopher

WWW access via:

http://www.cs.purdue.edu/coast/coast.html

Computer Security Publications from NIST—send e-mail to docserver@ csrc.ncsl.nist.gov with the message "send index" for a list of NIST computer security publications. To retrieve copies of the publication via e-mail, send message "send <document filename>. The NIST also distributes a Computer System Security Laboratory Newsletter via the Internet. Send e-mail message to mailserve@nist.gov with the message "subscribe csl-newsletter."

Computer Security Resource Clearinghouse (CSRC)—the NIST Computer Security Division maintains an electronic clearinghouse to encourage the sharing of information on computer security. The CSRC contains computer security awareness and training information, publications, conferences, and software tools, as well as security alerts and prevention measures. The CSRC system is available 24 hours a day, 7 days a week. NIST does not charge a usage fee for this service. To access the CSRC system via the Internet (http, gopher, and ftp). To connect via gopher and ftp, use the following: gopher csrc.ncsl.nist.gov or 129.6.54.11 ftp csrc.ncsl.nist.gov or 129.6.54.11. To access the clearinghouse via an http client, such as Mosaic, use the following Uniform Resource Locator (URL):

http://csrc.ncsl.nist.gov/

For users with Internet-accessible e-mail capability, send e-mail to: docserver@ncsl.nist.gov with the following message: send filename, where filename is the name of the file you wish to retrieve. Users can also use an http client by dialing into the CSRC at (301) 948-5717.

Cryptography, PGP, and Your Privacy Web Page—contains links to many of the Web's resources on cryptography, as well as lots of documentation on the Pretty Good Privacy (PGP) encryption program for pcs, Macs, and Unix. Contains a page of links to privacy related Web sources. The URL is:

http://draco.centerline.com:8080/~franl/crypto.html

CTI-CCC-AUDIT—Auditing and accounting mailing list sponsored by the CTI Centre for Accounting, Finance and Management at the School of Information Systems, University of East Anglia, U.K. The list is open to anyone interested in Auditing and wanting to be in contact with others with similar interests. This is a listserve and to subscribe send an e-mail message to mailbase@mailbase.ac.uk and state in the message Join cti-acc-audit Firstname Lastname

Department of Accounting, Finance, and Information Systems, University of Canterbury, Christchurch, New Zealand—this is a WWW site with subjects on accounting, finance, and information systems. The URL is:

http://www.afis.canterbury.ac.nz/afishome.html

FedWorld—over 135 Federal Government BBSs, including GAO Office of Policy BBS, Office of Management and Budget. Direct Dial Access (703)321-8020 Telnet Access Via Internet=fedworld.gov (192.239.92.3) FTP Site Access Via Internet=ftp.fedworld.gov (192.239.92.205) World Wide Web (Home Page)= www.fedworld.gov (this is the URL).

FinanceNet—network of professional governmental financial management organizations, agencies, and departments. Share information and ideas for improving financial management throughout all levels of government. Accountants, auditors, and financial managers participate and share financial management information, ideas, news, experiences, software, comments on financial documents, best practices, resources, etc. Gopher to FinanceNet@ financenet.gov. The URL for WWW is:

http://WWW.financenet.gov

FinanceNet Mailing Lists and a FinanceNet Newsgroup are now available. For more information on FinanceNet mailing lists send e-mail to e-mail-info@financenet.gov. Point your newsreader to news.financenet.gov for this new Usenet news group.

FinanceNet WWW Access—auditors with gopher access can reach the FinanceNet WWW site via telnet to one of several locations and logging in as "Lynx." This accesses most features of the Web except for graphics. FinanceNet will soon offer their own Lynx access. Lynx access is currently available as /Welcome to FinanceNet or /FinanceNet WWW Access via Lynx.

FINWeb—is the Financial Economics WWW server managed at the University of Texas at Austin. Provides a list of Internet resources with substantive information concerning economics and finance-related topics. Includes the Financial Economics Network, the Journal of Finance, the Financial Executive Journal, and Resources for Economists on the Internet. Also includes services such as EDGAR providing SEC reports and statements on publicly traded companies. The URL is:

http://finweb.bus.utexas.edu/finweb.html

Firewalls Mailing List—this is a listserve devoted to the subject of Firewalls and Internet Security. Any auditor concerned with Information Security and the issue of firewalls should subscribe to this list. The list generates a great deal of traffic on the subject of Internet security and the construction of firewalls. Subscriptions should be sent to Majordomo@GreatCircle.com with the message subscribe firewalls—digest. I would recommend the Digest version rather than the direct mail (non-digest) version.

Flowcharting BBS—Patton & Patton, makers of Flowcharting (software) provides on-line assistance to flowcharters via their bulletin board system. Registered users of Flowcharting by Patton & Patton should provide their serial number, which will allow access to files pertaining to your version. Limited access to the system is provided for auditors without a serial number. The BBS provides on-line technical support as well as the ability to share flowcharts or images. To reach the Patton & Patton BBS dial (408) 778-9697. While access to the BBS is free, users must remember that long-distance toll charges apply.

General Accounting Office of Policy's BBS—the GAO Office of Policy's BBS provides resources for government auditors, such as a Windows or DOS version of the Government Auditing Standards revised as of June 1994. The BBS also has the GAO's Policy and Procedures Manual available for download. The BBS is available via the Internet, on FedWorld, or directly via modem. The GAO Office of Policy's BBS phone number is (202) 512-4286.

Government Finance Officer's Association Mailing List—the GFOA has an electronic Internet mail list on FinanceNet. The GFOA will post announcements and other important information via this mailing list. For information on this and other FinanceNet mailing lists send e-mail to e-mail-info@financenet.gov. To post information to the GFOA mailing list, send message to GFOA@financenet.gov.

IAWWW—available, on a temporary and non-production basis, at URL: http://WW01.DHMC.DARTMOUTH.EDU/

The "01" in WW01 are numerics and *not* alpanumeric. The URL will be utilized until a production level ** .COM **Site becomes available.

IGNet—IGNet is an Internet-based electronic communications network dedicated to promoting excellence in the Inspector General community. Users collect and exchange information of interest to the IG community across a wide spectrum—federal, state, local, and foreign governments. It is designed to provide a wide array of resource and reference material in one central location. Research time can be reduced for persons conducting audits, inspections, or investigations through the effective use of pointers to other gopher servers containing valuable reference information. The IGNet gopher has moved from the Department of Justice to the Small Business Administration. This change was made to make administration of the gopher more accessible to the IGNet director and executive committee. The new address for the gopher is: <www.sbaonline.sba.gov>. This will put you in the main SBA gopher, which has a menu pick for IGNet. If you want to go directly to the IGNet screen, use the following URL:

<gopher://www.sbaonline.sba.gov:70/11/ignet>

IGNet Mailing List—IGNet distributes a number of mailing lists to the IG community. Audit-info is available to auditors based on prior registration and approval by the IGNet Coordinator. Interested parties must register with IGNet by e-mail to <jedye@fred.net>. Send the following registration information in the first message and save a round trip: name, organization, position, mailing address, voice number, fax number, and e-mail address. Upon approval, IGNet will send a welcome message telling about the features of IGNet, including the mailing lists and gopher.

Information Security Discussion List—INFSEC-L is a nonmoderated Internet discussion list intended to foster open and constructive communication among information security and auditing professionals in government, industry, and academic institutions. Discussion is encouraged on a broad range of topics and issues related to information security. Initial subscriptions to the list are screened by the listener to ensure addition of only appropriate individuals. Send subscription requests to listserv@etsuadmn.etsu.edu with one line in the body of the letter: SUB INFSEC-L yourname.

Information Systems Audit and Control Association—(ISACA—formerly EDPAA) Northeast Ohio Chapter BBS on the Cleveland Free-Net. Sysop—Ron Moritz. Direct modem: (216) 368-3888 (9600 v.32) or via the Internet using one of the following: telnet freenet-in-a.cwru.edu; telnet freenet-in-b.cwru.edu; telnet freenet-in-c.cwru.edu; 129.22.8.32; 129.22.8.51

Information Systems Audit and Control Association (ISACA) Listserve Mailing Lists—the following Chapters of ISACA have established listserve mailing lists:

The Central Indiana Chapter ISACA created a list for information systems auditors called CISACA-L. The list is meant to encourage professional discussion and is open to all information system auditors. To subscribe, send a one-line message to listserv@vm.cc.purdue.edu with the message SUBSCRIBE

CISACA-L (yourname). Messages sent to CISACA-L@vm.cc.purdue.edu will be distributed to all subscribers.

The New England Chapter ISACA created a list for information system auditors. The list is open and seeks to encourage professional discussions. To subscribe, send an e-mail message to listserv@mitvma.mit.edu and provide the following: SUBSCRIBE ISACA-L yourfirstname yourlastname.

The New Mexico Chapter of ISACA now has a home page on the World Wide Web. It includes information about meetings, professional development, conferences and the CISA program. The URL is:

http://www.cabq.gov/aud/isaca.html

Institute of Chartered Accountants of England and Wales Accounting Information Service—the ICAEW Summa Project is the site of the World Wide Web information server for accounting academics, students, and professionals. The project is funded by a grant from a research committee of the ICAEW. The WWW site is at the University of Exeter, Devon, U.K. It provides access to a number of accounting, auditing, and finance-related resources such as FINWeb, EDGAR, the Security and Exchange Commission's online database, the Financial Executive Journal, Global Network Navigator (source of information about Internet resources), and more. The URL for WWW is:

http://www.ex.ac.uk/~BJSpaul/ICAEW/ICAEW.html

For more information, send e-mail to the project director, Barry Spaul (bjspaul @ex.ac.uk).

Innovations Group BBS—contact Liz Diaz at (813) 622-8484. Prodigy Bulletin Board for local governments. Includes 130 individuals from more than 87 jurisdictions across the U.S.

Institute of Management Accountants (IMA) BBS—offers employment opportunities, bibliographies on new publications, catalog of publications, CMA exam information, continuing education information, news, articles, and a research forum. They are working on an international number as well as developing access to WWW or gopher. Access IMA BBS within North America at (800)229-1268 via modem.

Institute of Management and Administration (IOMA)—the leading publisher of business and management information. Each month, their newsletters bring actionable, productive articles to managers and executives in virtually every industry sector, all at the same high editorial standards that challenge the popular cliches that fail to address today's new and pressing problems. The Administration section includes an Accounting and Taxation category with links to a number of other sites mentioned in the ARL. The URL for the IOMA home page is:

http://ioma.com/ioma/

Internal Audit Newsgroup—(Alt.business.internal-audit) Internal audit newsgroup formed September 5, 1994, for discussion of internal auditing related subjects. Open forum to share ideas, proposals, experiences, hopes, fears, and vulnerabilities. Access via usenet newsreader or on America Online Internet Center or GO Usenet on CompuServe. Also now available via TAPNet.

Internet Bulletin for CPAs—new publication that the publisher describes as a "tool for CPAs to find out what is happening on the Internet, useful discussion groups, and what and where are the new resources for CPAs." To subscribe, call (800)834-1996 or send e-mail to sales@kentis.kent.oh.us.

Journal of Financial Abstracts—published by the Financial Economics Network and devoted to the electronic publishing of abstracts in research in financial economics and related topics. The JFA is free and distributed electronically via the Internet. To subscribe, send e-mail to Wayne Marr at MarrM@clemson.edu.

Local Government Online—the Innovations Group issues a quarterly newsletter called Local Government Online which highlights ways cities and counties are using electronic communication to improve productivity, save money, and provide excellent service to citizens.

MeasureNet—established by the Office of Personnel Management in support of the National Performance Review recommendation to improve the measurement of government performance. Current areas of discussion include outcome measures, customer service standards, benchmarking, human resources measurement, and network development. For information on MeasureNet contact Michael Reeder at reeder@tmn.com.

Minnesota Office of the Legislative Auditor (OLA)—web server for the Legislative Auditor's Office. The OLA server includes a history of the office and information about the Financial Audit Division and Program Evaluation Division. OLA also offers copies of audit reports, including a report on Performance Budgeting, and provides links to the Minnesota legislature gopher server and federal, state, and Internet Information resources of interest to auditors. The URL is:

http://www.auditor.leg.state.mn.us/

MuniNet Mailing List—FinanceNet mailing list targeted to municipal and township financial managers and clerks. The list will be a distribution and discussion list for issues relating to financial management of municipalities, townships, and counties within larger geopolitical jurisdictions. To subscribe, send e-mail to listproc@financenet.gov and include message "subscribe MuniNet (FirstName LastName)."

National Association of Local Government Auditors (NALGA)—is now accessible via the City of Albuquerque, New Mexico. Posting includes excerpts from the LGANewsletter, including audit report abstracts. Future postings will include office and committee listings, NALGA mission and objectives, and conference and training information. Excerpts from the NALGA newsletter will also be posted to FinanceNet. There is also a mailing list for NALGA members and other interested auditors available through FinanceNet. Send request to jkaplan@capaccess.org for addition to the NALGA list.

National Association of Purchasing Management (NAPM)—the Silicon Valley Chapter maintains a World Wide Web page on the Internet. It includes resources for purchasing and supply management professionals. Purchasing articles include topics such as Software Licensing Flexibility, Paperless Purchasing, and Getting Started With EDI. The site also includes a library collection of books, videos, and audio cassettes on purchasing, materials, operations, and business management. The URL is:

http://catalog.com/napmsv/

National Computer Security Association (NCSA) Forum Auditing Section— NCSA manages a CompuServe forum dedicated to computer security and ethics (GO NCSAFORUM), which can also be chosen from the main menu of this section. The NCSA established an Auditing Section of the forum on CompuServe. The Auditing Section provides the auditing profession with an on-line real time international communications forum for discussing auditing and audit-related security issues. Participants are encouraged to share resources, technical knowledge, professional standards, product information, ideas, audit reports, audit programs, training, and job opportunities. Send e-mail to 75300.2557@ compuserve.com.

National Intergovernmental Audit Forum Electronic Conference—NIAF Conference is available on the GAO Office of Policy's BBS. It provides a newsletter, bulletins, files, and message area for governmental auditors. Access GAO Office of Policy BBS and join Conference 5.

National Library of Australia Department of Finance—pilot project to provide Australian Government information from the Department of Finance. The Information Technology and Systems area includes IT Acquisition Council Guidelines as well as information on publications such as Implementing Financial Management Information Systems. For more information contact Michael Ledwidge at M.Ledwidge@nla.gov.au or Ian Barndt at Ian.Barndt@ finance.ausgovfinance.telememo.au.

NYCComptNet—the Office of the New York City Comptroller established an Internet connection in FinanceNet's state and local government section. NYC offers other localities ideas on how to improve their financial systems and reporting, internal controls, and performance measures via the Internet. Access FinanceNet's State and Local Government area for postings.

RISKWeb—information resource for academics and professionals interested in risk management and insurance issues. The RISKNet WWW server is a service of the RISKNet mailing list maintained at the University of Texas at Austin. The RISKNet mailing list provides individuals around the world with a forum for open discussion of Risk and Insurance issues. The URL is:

http://riskweb.bus.utexas.edu/riskweb.html

Rutgers Accounting Web (RAW) Site—located at Rutgers University and mirrors the ANet WWW site. RAW URL is:

http://www.rutgers.edu/Accounting/raw.htm

Software Publishers Association Forum—the Software Publishers Association (SPA) sponsors this forum to keep members of SPA, developers, and users of computer software aware of SPA activities and developments. Members of the SPA are available online to answer questions about publishing software, such as how to obtain a copyright for a newly developed program, and how to audit multiple computers for pirated programs. Available on CompuServe by typing GO SPAFORUM. The latest version of SPAudit and the SPAudit.Txt file are always available on CompuServe. To download the latest versions, once within CompuServe, type GO SPAFORUM and SPAudit will be contained in one of the libraries under "SPAudit." Version 3.1 of SPAudit was available as of 10/21/94.

TAPNet—The Tax Accounting and Professional Network BBS provides tax and accounting professionals a means to obtain feedback and share information with colleagues on taxes and accounting issues that confront them on a daily basis. The system provides relevant resource information to professionals that is valuable and easy to access. TAPNet now provides access to the alt.business.internal-audit Usenet newsgroup. Access by modem at (603) 585-9170. Telnet access will soon be available.

United States Code on the WWW—The United States Code is the official, subject-matter-order compilation of the Federal laws of a general and permanent nature that are currently in force. In accordance with Section 285b of Title 2 of the U.S. Code, the Code is compiled by the Office of the Law Revision Counsel of the United States House of Representatives. The Code is divided into 50 titles by subject matter. Each title is divided into sections. Sections within a title may be grouped together as subtitles, chapters, subchapters, parts, subparts, or divisions. Available from the House of Representatives Internet Library. The URL is:

http://www.pls.com:8001/his/usc.html

WAccnet—the Washington Accounting Network maintains a listing of accounting information and mailing lists as well as the AuditNet Resource List. The lists are available via anonymous ftp. For more information, send an e-mail to Earl Hall (earl@eskimo.org).

DISCLOSURE DATABASE

Learning Objectives

After completing this chapter, you should understand:

- The various software products available from Disclosure Incorporated.

- The student version of the Disclosure software and database optionally included with this text.

- How to conduct computerized research through the use of this software.

A prominent database to access information from SEC-filed documents is the *Disclosure SEC Database* prepared by Disclosure Incorporated. Disclosure Incorporated was founded in 1968 for the specific purpose of providing the most timely and accurate information on publicly traded companies. To keep up with major developments and to meet the ever-changing needs of their users, Disclosure has taken advantage of the latest computer and communications technologies in the development of the *Disclosure SEC Database*.

 This database contains information on over 11,000 public companies, including information covering annual balance sheets, income statements, cash flow statements, quarterly financial statements, and much more. The data are extracted from reports filed by companies with the Securities and Exchange Commission (SEC). The SEC's guidelines include, but are not limited to (1) companies that are listed on a national exchange or (2) companies whose securities are traded over-the-counter and have at least 500 shareholders of one class of stock and at least $5 million in assets. New companies are added after the appropriate registration statement has been filed with the SEC. The database contains information on active filers only, i.e., a company must have filed a report containing financial statements within the past 18 months in order to be included in the database. The following types of companies are excluded from the database by definition: management investment companies, real estate limited partnerships, and oil/gas drilling funds.

 The *Disclosure SEC Database* contains over 250 data items. Figure 7-1 illustrates a sample corporate record contained on the database at the time of this writing. The primary focus of the database is financial data extracted from the following public filings of an entity:

* *10-K*—Annual Business and Financial Report.
* *10-Q*—Quarterly Financial Report.
* *20-F*—10-K equivalent filed by non-U.S. registrants.
* *8-K*—Unscheduled Material Events Report.
* *Proxy Statement*—Lists directors, officers, remuneration, etc.
* *Registration Statement*—Financial and other information for new security offerings.
* *Annual Report to Shareholders*—The financial information reported by Disclosure is supplemented with textual information, including the full text of the Auditor's Report, the Management Discussion and Analysis section, the President's Letter from the Annual Report to Shareholders, and the full text of the financial footnotes from the 10-K. Over 60 discrete financial items are available for up to 10 years of annual data and up to 12 quarters of quarterly data. The financial line items are templated for standardization across industries.

The database is currently available via various on-line vendors or directly from Disclosure on CD-ROM. The CD-ROM version, *Compact D/SEC*, allows users to retrieve company records by searching on any of the over 250 data items via an easy-to-use menu-driven user interface and is updated monthly. Typical uses of the database include investment analysis, business case studies, portfolio management, prospect identification, competitive monitoring, executive recruitment, and generation of corporate background material.

Disclosure also produces three other databases on CD-ROM: *Compact D/Canada, Compact D/Worldscope,* and *Compact D/New Issues.* The *Canada* and *Worldscope* products provide corporate information for Canadian and other major international companies similar to that found in *Compact D/SEC. Compact D/New Issues* contains facts and figures extracted from registration statements, amendments, prospectuses, and supplements filed with the SEC.

Disclosure Incorporated has been very gracious in the development of a mini version of this comprehensive, interactive, menu-driven database for use with this text for the conduct of accounting and auditing research. Your personal copy of this database is optionally available with your text. The following section provides a sample record of a company included in the *Disclosure SEC Database.* Following the sample records are the basic instructions in using the software and accessing the data.

FIGURE 7-1 (continued)

Sample Corporate Record

Just one example of the more than 11,000 corporate records you'll receive on a single compact disc when you order **Compact D/SEC.** The following is a representation of the database elements found in each corporate record.

COMPANY SUMMARY

ABBOTT LABORATORIES
ONE ABBOTT PARK ROAD
ABBOTT PARK, IL 600643500
TELEPHONE: 7089376100

DISCLOSURE CO NO: A030000000
COMPANY STATUS: Active

EXCHANGE: NYS
TICKER SYMBOL: ABT
LOCATION OF INCORPORATION: IL

D-U-N-S NO: 001307602
CUSIP NO: 0000028241

FORTUNE NO: 0059
FORBES NO: SA118; AS236; PRO29; MV028

SIC CODES: 2834; 2833; 2835; 2844; 2879; 3841; 3845

DESCRIPTION OF BUSINESS: DISCOVERS, DEVELOPS, MANUFACTURES AND SELLS A DIVERSIFIED LINE OF HUMAN HEALTH CARE PRODUCTS INCLUDING PHARMA-CEUTICALS, PERSONAL CARE ITEMS, NUTRITIONALS, DIAGNOSTIC SYSTEMS, AND MEDICAL EQUIPMENT; AND PRODUCES AGRICULTURAL CHEMICALS.

CURRENT SHARES OUTSTANDING:	810,578,733	(SOURCE: 10Q 07/31/94)
SHARES HELD BY OFF & DIR:	4,289,161	(SOURCE: PROXY)
NUMBER OF SHAREHOLDERS:	82,947	(SOURCE: 10K)
NUMBER OF EMPLOYEES:	49,659	(SOURCE: 10K)

FISCAL YEAR END: 12/31

LATEST ANNUAL FINANCIAL DATA: 12/31/93

LATEST QUARTERLY FINANCIAL DATA: 06/30/94 (Q2)

FIGURE 7-1 (continued)

AUDITOR'S REPORT

AUDITOR: ARTHUR ANDERSEN & CO. (SOURCE: 10K)

UNQUALIFIED; EXPLANATION, ADOPTION OF SFAS 106 ACCOUNTING FOR POSTRETIREMENT BENEFITS OTHER THAN PENSIONS

ABBOTT LABORATORIES AND SUBSIDIARIES

REPORT OF INDEPENDENT PUBLIC ACCOUNTANTS

REPORT OF INDEPENDENT PUBLIC ACCOUNTANTS TO THE SHAREHOLDERS OF ABBOTT LABORATORIES:

We have audited the accompanying consolidated balance sheet of Abbott Laboratories (an Illinois corporation) and Subsidiaries as of December 31, 1993, 1992, and 1991, and the related consolidated statements of earnings, shareholders' investment, and cash flows for the years then ended. These financial statements are the responsibility of the Company's management. Our responsibility is to express an opinion on these financial statements based on our audits.

We conducted our audits in accordance with generally accepted auditing standards. Those standards require that we plan and perform the audit to obtain reasonable assurance about whether the financial statements are free of material misstatement. An audit includes examining, on a test basis, evidence supporting the amounts and disclosures in the financial statements. An audit also includes assessing the accounting principles used and significant estimates made by management, as well as evaluating the overall financial statement presentation. We believe that our audits provide a reasonable basis for our opinion.

In our opinion, the financial statements referred to above present fairly, in all material respects, the financial position of Abbott Laboratories and Subsidiaries as of December 31, 1993, 1992, and 1991, and the results of their operations and their cash flows for the years then ended in conformity with generally accepted accounting principles.

As explained in Note 3 to the consolidated financial statements, the Company adopted the requirements of Statement of Financial Accounting Standards No. 106, "Employers' Accounting for Postretirement Benefits Other Than Pensions," effective January 1, 1991. Arthur Andersen & Co. Chicago, Illinois, January 14, 1994

LEGAL COUNSEL: NA

STOCK TRANSFER AGENT: FIRST NATIONAL BANK OF BOSTON

SEGMENT DATA ($000s)

(SOURCE: 10K 12/31/93)	SALES	OP INCOME
PHARMACEUTICAL AND NUTRITIONAL	4,389,000	1,211,000
HOSPITAL AND LABORATORY	4,019,000	794,000

FIVE YEAR SUMMARY

YEAR	SALES ($000s)	NET INCOME	EPS($)
1993	8,407,800	1,399,100	1.69
1992	7,851,900	1,239,100	1.47
1991	6,876,600	1,088,700	1.27

FIGURE 7-1 (continued)

1990	6,158,700	965,800	1.11
1989	5,379,800	859,800	0.96
Growth Rate (%)	11.8	12.9	15.1

FINANCIAL STATEMENTS

BALANCE SHEET
ANNUAL ASSETS ($000s)

FISCAL YEAR ENDING	12/31/93	12/31/92	12/31/91 . . .	12/31/85
CASH	300,676	115,576	60,395	313,714
MARKETABLE SECURITIES	78,149	141,601	85,838	123,744
RECEIVABLES	1,336,222	1,244,396	1,150,894	563,316
INVENTORIES	940,533	863,808	815,385	463,793
RAW MATERIALS	247,492	251,713	222,768	129,261
WORK IN PROGRESS	216,493	190,163	186,591	94,331
FINISHED GOODS	476,548	421,932	406,026	240,201
NOTES RECEIVABLE	NA	NA	NA	NA
OTHER CURRENT ASSETS	929,955	865,357	778,556	215,831
TOTAL CURRENT ASSETS	3,585,535	3,231,738	2,891,068	1,680,398
GROSS PROPERTY, PLANT & EQ	6,221,146	5,497,141	4,785,223	2,075,661
ACCUMULATED DEPRECIATION	2,710,155	2,397,903	2,123,140	707,119
NET PROPERTY, PLANT & EQ	3,510,991	3,099,238	2,662,083	1,368,542
INVESTMENT & ADV TO SUBS	221,815	270,639	340,184	281,063
OTHER NON CURRENT ASSETS	NA	NA	NA	NA
DEFERRED CHARGES (ASSET)	370,228	339,621	361,931	138,170
INTANGIBLES	NA	NA	NA	NA
DEPOSITS & OTHER ASSETS	NA	NA	NA	NA
TOTAL ASSETS	7,688,569	6,941,236	6,255,266	3,468,373

ANNUAL LIABILITIES ($000s)

FISCAL YEAR ENDING	12/31/93	12/31/92	12/31/91 . . .	12/31/85
NOTES PAYABLE	841,541	909,116	523,526	112,508
ACCOUNTS PAYABLE	638,509	597,226	522,397	204,036
CURRENT LONG TERM DEBT	2,080	7,147	20,724	10,351
CURR PORTION OF CAP LEASES	NA	NA	NA	NA
ACCRUED EXPENSES	1,148,481	1,102,136	862,138	322,911
INCOME TAXES	324,749	41,583	194,255	96,860
OTHER CURRENT LIABILITIES	139,600	125,300	106,297	41,800
TOTAL CURRENT LIABILITIES	3,094,933	2,782,508	2,229,337	788,466
MORTGAGES	NA	NA	NA	NA
DEFERRED CHARGES (LIAB)	51,383	321,301	347,245	252,141
CONVERTIBLE DEBT	NA	NA	NA	NA
LONG TERM DEBT	306,840	110,018	125,118	442,953
NON CURRENT CAPITAL LEASES	NA	NA	NA	NA
OTHER LONG TERM LIAB	560,484	379,768	350,579	114,150

FIGURE 7-1 (continued)

TOTAL LIABILITIES	4,013,640	3,593,595	3,052,279	1,597,710
MINORITY INTEREST (LIAB)	NA	NA	NA	NA
PREFERRED STOCK	NA	NA	NA	NA
COMMON STOCK NET	469,828	442,390	361,008	185,879
CAPITAL SURPLUS	NA	NA	NA	NA
RETAINED EARNINGS	3,364,952	2,990,689	2,867,857	1,844,200
TREASURY STOCK	51,783	52,593	54,024	103,394
OTHER LIABILITIES	−108,068	−32,845	28,146	−56,022
SHAREHOLDERS EQUITY	3,674,929	3,347,641	3,202,987	1,870,663
TOTAL LIAB & NET WORTH	7,688,569	6,941,236	6,255,266	3,468,373

ANNUAL INCOME STATEMENT ($000s)

FISCAL YEAR ENDING	12/31/93	12/31/92	12/31/91 . . .	12/31/85
NET SALES	8,407,843	7,851,912	6,876,588	3,360,273
COST OF GOODS	3,684,727	3,505,273	3,139,972	1,694,934
GROSS PROFIT	4,723,116	4,346,639	3,736,616	1,665,339
R&D EXPENDITURES	880,974	772,407	666,336	240,584
SELL, GENERAL & ADMIN EXP	1,918,176	2,048,220	1,513,250	687,608
INCOME BEFORE DEPR & AMORT	1,923,966	1,526,012	1,557,030	737,147
DEPRECIATION & AMORT	NA	NA	NA	NA
NON OPERATING INCOME	73,547	265,702	51,023	55,478
INTEREST EXPENSE	54,283	52,961	63,831	98,095
INCOME BEFORE TAXES	1,943,230	1,738,753	1,544,222	694,530
PROVISION FOR INCOME TAXES	544,104	499,696	455,545	229,195
MINORITY INTEREST INCOME	NA	NA	NA	NA
INVESTMENT GAINS	NA	NA	NA	NA
OTHER INCOME	NA	NA	NA	NA
NET INCOME BEFORE EX ITEMS	1,399,126	1,239,057	1,088,677	465,335
EX ITEMS & DISCONTINUED OP	NA	NA	68	NA
NET INCOME	1,399,126	1,239,057	1,088,745	465,335
OUTST SHARES (NOT IN 000s)	821,129,684	836,052,429	850,529,226	39,190,768

CASH FLOW STATEMENT

CASH FLOW PROVIDED BY OPERATING ACTIVITY ($000s)

FISCAL YEAR ENDING	12/31/93	12/31/92 . . .	12/31/91
Net Income (Loss)	1,399,126	1,239,057	1,088,745
Depreciation/Amortization	484,081	427,782	379,017
Net Incr(Decr) Assets(Liab)	2,055	282,440	61,768
Cash Prov(Used) in Disc Op	NA	NA	4,015
Oth Adjustments, Net	34,243	4,450	43,200
Net Cash Prov(Used) by Op	1,846,909	1,388,849	1,453,209

CASH FLOW PROVIDED BY INVESTING ACTIVITY ($000s)

(Incr)Decr in Prop, Plant	952,732	1,007,247	770,611
(Acq)Disp Subs, Business	NA	NA	NA
Incr(Decr) in Investments	112,068	317,393	114,590
Oth Cash Inflows(Outflows)	46,826	22,277	13,915
Net Cash Prov(Used) by Inv	793,838	667,577	642,106

FIGURE 7-1 (continued)

CASH FLOW PROVIDED BY FINANCING ACTIVITY ($000s)

Issue(Purchase) Equity	438,286	533,571	259,913
Issue(Repayment) Debt	NA	NA	NA
Inc(Decr) Bank, Oth Brwng	122,413	364,502	109,564
Dividends, Oth Distribs	548,044	488,413	410,345
Other Cash Inflows(Outflows)	NA	NA	NA
Net Cash Prov(Used) by Fin	863,867	657,482	779,822
Eff of Exchg Rate on Cash	5,104	7,609	4,920
Net Change Cash or Equiv	184,100	56,181	26,361
Cash or Equiv Beg of Year	116,576	60,395	34,034
Cash or Equiv End of Year	300,676	116,576	60,395

INCOME STATEMENT FULL TEXT

SOURCE: 10K 12/31/93

Abbott Laboratories and Subsidiaries

CONSOLIDATED STATEMENT OF EARNINGS

(Dollars in Thousands Except Per Share Data)

Year Ended December 31	1993	1992
Net Sales	8,407,843	7,851,912
Cost of products sold	3,684,727	3,505,273
Research and development	880,974	772,407
Selling, general and administrative	1,988,176	1,833,220
Provision for product withdrawal	70,000	215,000
Total Operating Cost and Expenses	6,483,877	6,325,900
Operating Earnings	1,923,966	1,526,012
Interest expense	54,283	52,961
Interest and dividend income	37,821	42,250
Other (income) expense, net	35,726	48,534
Gain on sale of investment	271,986	
Earnings Before Taxes	1,943,230	1,738,753
Taxes on earning	544,104	499,696
Earnings Before Extraordinary Gain and Accounting Change	1,399,126	1,239,057
Extraordinary Gain, Net of Tax of $74,068		
Cumulative Effect of Accounting Change, Net of Tax of $78,151		
Net Earnings	1,399,126	1,239,057
Earnings Per Common Share Before		
Extraordinary Gain and Accounting Change	1.69	1.47
Extraordinary Gain, Net of Tax		
Cumulative Effect of Accounting Change, Net of Tax		
Earnings Per Common Share	1.69	1.47
Average Number of Common Shares Outstanding	828,988,000	44,122,000

The accompanying notes to consolidated financial statements are an integral part of this statement.

FIGURE 7-1 (continued)

BALANCE SHEET ASSETS FULL TEXT

SOURCE: 10K 12/31/93

Abbott Laboratories and Subsidiaries

CONSOLIDATED BALANCE SHEET

(Dollars in Thousands)
December 31

Assets	1993	1992
Current Assets:		
Cash and cash equivalents	300,676	116,576
Investment securities, at cost	78,149	141,601
Trade receivables, less allowances of 1993: $116,925; 1992: $106,857; 1991: $82,244	1,336,222	1,244,396
Inventories		
Finished products	476,548	421,932
Work in process	216,493	190,163
Materials	247,492	251,713
Total inventories	940,533	863,808
Prepaid income taxes	458,026	477,387
Other prepaid expenses and receivables	471,929	387,970
Total Current Assets	3,585,535	3,231,738
Investment Securities Maturing After One Year, at Cost	221,815	270,639
Property And Equipment, at cost:		
Land	137,636	120,617
Buildings	1,261,620	1,064,974
Equipment	4,169,279	3,735,259
Construction in progress	652,611	576,291
	6,221,146	5,497,141
Less: accumulated depreciation and amortization	2,710,155	2,397,903
Net Property and Equipment	3,510,991	3,099,238
Deferred Charges and Other Assets	370,228	339,621
	7,688,569	6,941,236

The accompanying notes to consolidated financial statements are an integral part of this statement.

BALANCE SHEET LIABILITIES FULL TEXT

SOURCE: 10K 12/31/93

Abbott Laboratories and Subsidiaries

FIGURE 7-1 (continued)

Liabilities and Shareholders' Investment	1993	1992
Current Liabilities:		
Shortterm borrowings	841,514	909,116
Trade accounts payable	638,509	597,226
Salaries, wages and commissions	215,432	196,259
Other accrued liabilities	933,049	905,877
Dividends payable	139,600	125,300
Income taxes payable	324,749	41,583
Current portion of longterm debt	2,080	7,147
Total Current Liabilities	3,094,933	2,782,508
LongTerm Debt	306,840	110,018
Other Liabilities and Deferrals:		
Deferred income taxes	51,383	321,301
Other	560,484	79,768
Total Other Liabilities and Deferrals	611,867	701,069
Shareholders' Investment		
Preferred shares, one dollar per value Authorized 1,000,000 shares, none issued		
Common shares, without par value Authorized 1,200,000,000 shares; Issued at stated capital amount 1993: 830,941,641 shares; 1992: 846,017,815 shares; 1991: 860,765,782 shares	469,828	442,390
Earnings employed in the business	3,364,952	2,990,689
Cumulative translation adjustments	100,716	23,131
	3,734,064	3,409,948
Less:		
Common shares held in treasury, at cost 1993: 9,811,930 shares; 1992: 9,965,386 shares; 1991: 10,236,556 shares	51,783	52,593
Unearned compensation restricted stock awards	7,352	9,714
Total Shareholders' Investment	3,674,929	3,347,641
	7,688,569	6,941,236

COMMENTS:

DEFERRED CHARGES INCLUDE OTHER ASSETS (10Q 03-31-92) (10Q 06-30-93) (10Q 09-30-93) (10K 12-31-93) (10Q 03-31-94) (10Q 06-30-94)

ACCRUED EXPENSES INCLUDE INCOME TAXES (10Q 03-31-94)

NOTES PAYABLE INCLUDE CURRENT PORTION OF LONGTERM DEBT (10Q 03-31-93) (10Q 06-30-93) (10Q 09-30-93) (10Q 03-31-94) (10Q 06-30-94)

OTHER EQUITY REPRESENTS CUMULATIVE TRANSLATION ADJUSTMENT AND UNEARNED COMPENSATION (10Q 03-31-93) (10Q 06-30-93) (10Q 09-30-93) (10K 12-31-93) (10Q 03-31-94) (10Q 06-30-94)

EXTRAORDINARY ITEMS REPRESENT CUMULATIVE EFFECT OF ACCOUNTING CHANGE AND GAIN ON SALE OF INVESTMENT IN 1991

FIVE YEAR SUMMARY NET INCOME AND EARNINGS PER SHARE ARE BEFORE EXTRAORDINARY GAIN AND ACCOUNTING CHANGE

FIGURE 7-1 (continued)

BALANCE SHEET
QUARTERLY ASSETS ($000s)

FOR QUARTER ENDING	06/30/94	03/31/94	12/31/93	... 09/30/91
CASH	180,596	171,063	300,676	49,483
MARKETABLE SECURITIES	68,477	36,543	78,149	149,450
RECEIVABLES	1,433,592	1,350,307	1,336,222	1,042,347
INVENTORIES	1,052,449	983,239	940,533	801,686
RAW MATERIALS	270,871	249,892	247,492	209,519
WORK IN PROGRESS	222,749	224,006	216,493	190,667
FINISHED GOODS	558,829	509,341	476,548	401,500
NOTES RECEIVABLE	NA	NA	NA	NA
OTHER CURRENT ASSETS	986,730	979,332	929,955	674,279
TOTAL CURRENT ASSETS	3,721,844	3,520,484	3,585,535	2,717,245
GROSS PROPERTY, PLANT & EQ	6,623,611	6,407,647	6,221,146	4,568,033
ACCUMULATED DEPRECIATION	2,938,531	2,823,906	2,710,155	2,048,328
NET PROPERTY, PLANT & EQ	3,685,080	3,583,741	3,510,991	2,519,705
INVESTMENT & ADV TO SUBS	272,380	289,563	221,815	293,282
OTHER NON CURRENT ASSETS	NA	NA	NA	NA
DEFERRED CHARGES (ASSET)	403,632	353,628	370,228	338,086
INTANGIBLES	NA	NA	NA	NA
DEPOSITS & OTHER ASSETS	NA	NA	NA	NA
TOTAL ASSETS	8,082,936	7,747,416	7,688,569	5,868,318

QUARTERLY LIABILITIES ($000s)

FOR QUARTER ENDING	6/30/94	03/31/94	12/31/93	... 09/30/91
NOTES PAYABLE	745,798	675,432	841,514	532,950
ACCOUNTS PAYABLE	724,472	602,829	638,509	363,545
CURRENT LONG TERM DEBT	NA	NA	2,080	NA
CURR PORTION OF CAP LEASES	NA	NA	NA	NA
ACCRUED EXPENSES	1,798,725	1,775,869	1,148,481	1,166,913
INCOME TAXES	NA	NA	324,749	NA
OTHER CURRENT LIABILITIES	NA	NA	139,600	NA
TOTAL CURRENT LIABILITIES	3,268,995	3,054,130	3,094,933	2,063,408
MORTGAGES	NA	NA	NA	NA
DEFERRED CHARGES (LIAB)	NA	NA	51,383	NA
CONVERTIBLE DEBT	NA	NA	NA	NA
LONG TERM DEBT	307,275	306,855	306,840	132,229
NON CURRENT CAPITAL LEASES	NA	NA	NA	NA
OTHER LONG TERM LIAB	650,486	634,673	560,484	661,261
TOTAL LIABILITIES	4,226,756	3,995,658	4,013,640	2,856,898
MINORITY INTEREST (LIAB)	NA	NA	NA	NA
PREFERRED STOCK	NA	NA	NA	NA
COMMON STOCK NET	492,165	480,310	469,828	328,305
CAPITAL SURPLUS	NA	NA	NA	NA
RETAINED EARNINGS	3,491,873	3,422,903	3,364,952	2,736,894
TREASURY STOCK	51,743	51,783	51,783	54,098
OTHER LIABILITIES	−76,115	−99,672	−108,068	319
SHAREHOLDERS' EQUITY	3,856,180	3,751,758	3,674,929	3,011,420
TOTAL LIAB & NET WORTH	8,082,936	7,747,416	7,688,569	5,868,318

FIGURE 7-1 (continued)

QUARTERLY INCOME STATEMENT ($000s)

FOR QUARTER ENDING	06/30/94	03/31/94	12/31/93	. . . 09/30/91
NET SALES	2.204,030	2,215,248	2,227,997	1,653,693
COST OF GOODS	946,816	964,272	947,492	767,073
GROSS PROFIT	1,257,214	1,250,976	1,280,505	886,620
R&D EXPENDITURES	244,989	226,797	241,363	172,793
SELL, GENERAL & ADMIN EXP	468,739	497,184	495,166	361,273
INCOME BEFORE DEPR & AMORT	543,486	526,995	543,976	352,554
DEPRECIATION & AMORT	NA	NA	NA	NA
NON OPERATING INCOME	6,703	7,692	12,309	17,805
INTEREST EXPENSE	12,253	11,496	12,828	13,535
INCOME BEFORE TAXES	537,936	523,191	543,457	356,824
PROVISION FOR INCOME TAXES	161,381	156,957	152,168	105,263
MINORITY INTEREST INCOME	NA	NA	NA	NA
INVESTMENT GAINS	NA	NA	NA	NA
OTHER INCOME	NA	NA	NA	NA
NET INCOME BEFORE EX ITEMS	365,555	366,234	391,289	251,561
EX ITEMS & DISCONTINUED OP	NA	NA	NA	NA
NET INCOME	376,555	366,234	391,289	251,561
OUTST SHARES (NOT IN 000s)	812,169,314	816,643,245	821,129,684	425,693,107

MARKET DATA

WEEKLY DATA
PRICE INFORMATION

FOR WEEK ENDING	10/20/94
LATEST TRADE DATE	10/20/94
OUTSTANDING SHARES (000s)	810,579
VOLUME	5,733,300
HIGH (OR ASKED) PRICE	32.000
LOW (OR BID) PRICE	30.250
CLOSE (OR AVERAGE) PRICE	31.250

EARNINGS INFORMATION

DATE FOR 12 MONTHS ENDING	09/94
EARNINGS PER SHARE (EPS)	1.820
PRICE/EARNINGS RATIO	17.170

DIVIDEND INFORMATION

	CURRENT	PREVIOUS
INDICATED ANNUAL DIVIDEND	00.760	
CURRENT DIVIDEND	00.1900	00.1900
EXDIVIDEND DATE	10/07/94	07/11/94
RECORD DATE	10/14/94	07/15/94
PAYABLE DATE	11/15/94	08/15/94
PAYMENT METHOD	U.S. CURRENCY	U.S. CURRENCY

FIGURE 7-1 (continued)

I/B/E/S: EARNINGS ESTIMATES

PERIOD	EPS EST'S				CHG IN MEAN(S):	
	Mean	High	Low	Number of Ests	1 Month	3 Month
FY 12/94	1.86	1.90	1.75	30	0.00	0.00
FY 12/95	2.09	2.15	1.80	30	0.00	0.00
QTR 12/94	0.53	0.54	0.51	20	0.00	0.00
QTR 3/95	0.51	0.53	0.49	11	0.00	0.00

EARNINGS PER SHARE ANNUAL GROWTH RATES

Last 5 Years	14.8%
Next 5 Years	12.3%
FY94/93	10.2%
FY95/94	12.3%
QTR 12/94	10.6%
QTR 3/95	12/5%

ABT Abbott Labs
Industry Code: DRUGS
Price $32.13

Period	EPS	P/E	P/E : S&P	P/E : IND	Dividend	Yield
FY12/93	1.69				0.76	2.4%
FY12/94	*1.86	17.2	1.11	1.00		*2.4%
FY12/95	*2.09	15.4	1.09	0.91		*2.4%

*Estimated

	FCST EPS GROWTH			RELATIVE	
	ABT	IND	S&P 500	ABT to IND	ABT to S&P
FY94 vs FY93	10.2%	10.2%	15.4%	100	66
FY95 vs FY94	12.3%	11.5%	18.8%	107	65
Next 5 Years	12.3%	11.4%	11.7%	108	105
Last 5 Years	14.8%	11.6%	7.0%	128	212
PE FY 1994	17.2	17.3	15.6	100	111
PE FY 1995	15.4	17.0	14.1	91	109

FIGURE 7-1 (continued)

DISTRIBUTION OF EPS ESTS. AS OF 12/15/94

ABT EPS FY 12/93 $1.69

FY 12/94   FY 12/95
30 ESTS   30 ESTS
MEAN EPS $1.86   MEAN EPS $2.09

```
            X                                                    X
            X                                                    X
            X   X                                                X
            XXRX                                               X   X
            XXXX                                               X   X
            XXXX  X                                            X   X
            XXXX  X                                        X   XXX
    X    X XXXXXX                            X             XXXXX
+ - - - - + - - - - - + - - - - - +          + - - - - - + - - - - - + - - - - - +
$1.70    1.80      1.90    2.00              $1.60    1.80      2.00    2.20
```
X=EST R/L=RAISED/LOWERED PAST MO.   N=NEW PAST MO.   *=9+ESTS

RATIOS

KEY ANNUAL FINANCIAL RATIOS

FISCAL YEAR ENDING	12/31/93	12/31/92	12/31/91
QUICK RATIO	0.55	0.54	0.58
CURRENT RATIO	1.16	1.16	1.30
NET SALES/CASH	22.19	30.41	47.02
SG&A EXPENSE/SALES	0.23	0.26	0.22
RECEIVABLES TURNOVER	6.29	6.31	5.97
RECEIVABLES DAY SALES	57.21	57.05	60.25
INVENTORY TURNOVER	8.94	9.09	8.43
INVENTORY DAY SALES	40.27	39.60	42.69
NET SALES/WORKING CAPITAL	17.14	17.48	10.39
NET SALES/NET PLANT & EQ	2.39	2.53	2.58
NET SALES/CURRENT ASSETS	2.34	2.43	2.38
NET SALES/TOTAL ASSETS	1.09	1.13	1.10
NET SALES/EMPLOYEES	169,312	163,180	150,492
TOTAL LIAB/TOTAL ASSETS	0.52	0.52	0.49
TOTAL LIAB/INVESTED CAP	1.01	1.04	0.92
TOTAL LIAB/COMMON EQUITY	1.09	1.07	0.95
TIMES INTEREST EARNED	36.80	33.83	25.19
CURRENT DEBT/EQUITY	0.00	0.00	0.01
LONG TERM DEBT/EQUITY	0.08	0.03	0.04
TOTAL DEBT EQUITY	0.08	0.03	0.05
TOTAL ASSETS/EQUITY	2.09	2.07	1.95
PRETAX INCOME/NET SALES	0.23	0.22	0.22
PRETAX INCOME/TOTAL ASSETS	0.25	0.25	0.25
PRETAX INCOME/INVESTED CAP	0.49	0.50	0.46
PRETAX INCOME/COMMON EQ	0.53	0.52	0.48

FIGURE 7-1 (continued)

NET INCOME/NET SALES	0.17	0.16	0.16
NET INCOME/TOTAL ASSETS	0.18	0.18	0.17
NET INCOME/INVESTED CAP	0.35	0.36	0.33
NET INCOME/COMMON EQUITY	0.38	0.37	0.34
R&D EXPENDITURES/NET SALES	0.10	0.10	0.10
R&D EXPENDITURES/NET INC.	0.63	0.62	0.61
R&D EXPENDITURES/EMPLOYEES	17,740.00	16,052.00	14,583.00

OFFICERS AND DIRECTORS

Officers (Name/Age/Title/Remuneration):

(SOURCE: 10K)

BURNHAM, DUANE L / 52 / CHAIRMAN OF THE BOARD, CHIEF EXECUTIVE OFFICER / $2,501,870

HODGSON, THOMAS R. / 52 / PRESIDENT, CHIEF OPERATING OFFICER / $1,711,539

CLARK, PAUL N. / 47 / SENIOR VICE PRESIDENT / $711,466

COUGHLAN, GARY P. / 49 / SENIOR VICE PRESIDENT, CHIEF FINANCIAL OFFICER / $795,232

THOMPSON, DAVID A. / 52 / SENIOR VICE PRESIDENT (PRX 030494) / $784,595

-
-
-

WALVOORD, ELLEN M. / 54 / VICE PRESIDENT / NA

WENDLER, JOSEF / 44 / VICE PRESIDENT / NA

WHITE, MILES D. / 38 / VICE PRESIDENT / NA

WRIGHT, DON G. / 51 / VICE PRESIDENT / NA

DIRECTORS / NOMINEES (NAME / AGE /TITLE / REMUNERATION):

(SOURCE: PROXY 03/04/94)

AUSTEN, K. FRANK / 65 / NOMINEE / NA

BURNHAM, DUANE L. / 52 / CHAIRMAN OF THE BOARD, CHIEF EXECUTIVE OFFICER, NOMINEE / $2,501,870

FULLER, H. LAURANCE / 55*T/ NOMINEE / NA

-
-
-

REYNOLDS, W. ANN / 56 / NOMINEE / NA

SMITHBURT, WILLIAM D. / 55 / NOMINEE / NA

WALTER, JOHN R. / 47 / NOMINEE / NA

WEISS, WILLIAM L. / 64 / NOMINEE / NA

Chapter 7

FIGURE 7-1 (continued)

OWNERSHIP

TYPE	DATE(Q,M)	OWNERS	CHANGE (000$)	HELD	%OWN
INSTITUTIONS	6/30/94(Q)	632	4,250	406,658	49.80
5% OWNERS	09/30/94(M)	2	NA	121,303	14.87
INSIDERS	08/31/94(M)	51	NA	4,517	0.55

CDA/SPECTRUM 13F INSTITUTIONAL OWNERSHIP

INSTITUTIONAL HOLDER	RANK	LATEST QTR CHC IN SHS	SHARES HELD	FILING DATE
WELLS FARGO INST. TR NA	1	−90,052	15,845,255	09/30/94
MORGAN J P & CO INC	2	1,305,225	15,137,971	09/30/90
BANKERS TRUST N Y CORP	3	−25,277	14,701,969	09/30/94
INVESCO CAPITAL MGMT INC	4	3,453	13,624,182	09/30/94
MELLON BANK CORPORATION	5	−717,171	12,315,372	09/30/94
NORTHERN TRUST CORP	6	−38,947	11,968,525	09/30/94
SAROFIM FAYEZ	7	−547,575	10,928,692	09/30/94
EQUITABLE COMPANIES INC	8	−1,131,581	10,204,336	09/30/94
WELLINGTON MANAGEMENT CO	9	341,690	8,544,600	09/30/94
AGGREGATE OF 423 OWNERS	NA	−5,654,853	25,478,236	NA
STATE STREET BOSTON CORP	10	−3,001,801	7,865,482	09/30/94
COLLEGE RETIRE EQUITES	11	−97,000	7,239,721	09/30/94
HARRIS BANKCORP INC.	12	25,924	7,163,287	09/30/94
NEW YORK ST TEACHERS RET	13	0	5,954,400	09/30/94
STATE FARM MUT AUTO INS	14	0	5,913,600	09/30/94
STATE STREET RESR & MGMT	15	1,183,500	5,309,324	09/30/94
KEYCORP	16	−663,406	5,145,594	09/30/94
DEAN WITTER DISCOVER&CO	17	79,822	5,047,732	09/30/94
•				
•				
•				
ASSOCIATED BANC-CORP	209	6,000	249,661	09/30/94
INVESCO MGMT & RES INC	210	−54,690	246,741	09/30/94
ROYAL LONDON MUTUAL INS	211	0	244,000	09/30/94
THIRD NATL BANK/NASHVLLE	212	−1,000	237,874	09/30/94
FIRST OF AMERICA BANK	213	−12,127	236,809	09/30/94
PIPER CAPTIAL MGMT INC	214	−6,508	235,998	09/30/94
PANAGORA ASSET MGMT INC	215	−28,100	234,500	09/30/94
CULLEN/FOREST BANKERS INC	216	−22,580	232,871	09/30/94
CRESTAR BANK/VIRGINIA	217	4,103	230,399	09/30/94
SWISS REINSURANCE CO	218	17,500	229,500	09/30/94
HOTCHKISS ASSOCIATES INC	219	−100	228,260	09/30/94
MERIDIAN BANCORP INC.	220	−4,300	226,647	09/30/94
SUNBANDS INC	221	−94,662	225,813	09/30/94
ST PAUL COMPANIES INC	222	56,000	223,000	09/30/94
COMMERCIAL NATL/SHREVEPT	223	−36,600	220,740	09/30/94

FIGURE 7-1 (continued)

MERCANTILE BANKSHARES CO	224	−9,202	220,592	09/30/94
FRANKLIN RESOURCES INC	225	−2,500	217,700	09/30/94
MILLER ANDERSON&SHERRERD	226	−4,700	217,400	09/30/94
MACKAY SHIELDS FINANCIAL	227	−19,875	215,000	09/30/94
FIRST MARYLAND BANCORP	228	8,000	214,091	09/30/94
NICHOLS & PRATT	229	300	211,700	09/30/94
TOTAL OF 631 OWNERS		−2,526,906	402,606,720	
MARKET VALUE ($MILLIONS)			12,634	09/30/94

CDA/SPECTRUM 5% BENEFICIAL OWNERSHIP

NAME OF OWNER	LOCATION	SHARES HELD	DATE	FORM
ABBOTT LABS STK RETIRE TR ETAL	UAS	62,315,816	12/31/92	13G
BURNHAM DUANE L ET AL	USA	58,987,496	12/31/89	13G
TOTAL OF 2 OWNERS		121,303,312		

CDA/SPECTRUM INSIDER OWNERSHIP

NAME OF INSIDER	RELATION-SHIP	RANK	LATEST TRADE	SHARES HELD	FILING DATE
SCHOELLHORN ROBERT A	D	1	0	1,449,496	03/90
BURNHAM DUANE L	CB	2	−50,000	436,629	12/93
HODGSON THOMAS R	P	3	0	319,438	12/92
•					
•					
•					
KRINGEL MARTHA ESTATE TRU T		50	0	4,800	05/92
RAND ADDISON BARRY	D	51	0	3,130	04/93
RAND ADDISON B	D	52	400	1,340	04/93
TOTAL OF 52 OWNERS			−290,203	4,542,408	

SUBSIDIARIES

ABBOTT BIOTECH, INC.
ABBOTT CHEMICALS, INC.
ABBOTT HEALTH PRODUCTS, INC.
ABBOTT HOME INFUSION SERVICES OF NEW YORK, INC.
ABBOTT INTERNATIONAL LTD.
ABBOTT INTERNATIONAL LTS. OF PUERTO RICO
•
•
•
ABBOTT LABORATORIES LTD. (THAILAND)
ABBOTT LABORATUARLARI ITHALAT IHRACAT VE TECARET ANONIM SIRKETI
ABBOTT LABORATORIES URUGUAY LTDA
ABBOTT LABORATORIES, CA (VENEZUELA)
MEDICAMENTOS M & R, SA

FIGURE 7-1 (continued)

FILINGS AND FULL-TEXT INFORMATION

FILINGS

06/30/94	10Q
04/29/94	PROXY
04/29/94	PROXY PLM
03/31/94	10Q
•	
•	
•	
06/30/93	10Q
03/31/93	10Q
04/21/92	LIS NYS

EXHIBITS

3.1 ARTICLES OF INCORPORATION ABBOTT LABORATORIES, INC BY REF TO THE FORM 10K (THE "1992 FORM 10K")

3.2 CORPORATE BYLAWS ABBOTT LABORATORIES, INC BY REF AS EXHIBIT 3 FOR THE QUARTER ENDED 6/30/93 ON FORM 10Q (THE "6/30/93 FORM 10Q")

10.1 SUPPLEMENTAL PLAN—ABBOTT LABORATORIES EXTENDED DISABILITY PLAN, INC BY REF TO THE 1992 FORM 10K

•

•

•

21 SUBSIDIARIES OF ABBOTT LABORATORIES

23.1 SUPPLEMENTAL REPORT OF INDEPENDENT PUBLIC ACCOUNTANTS

23.2 CONSENT OF INDEPENDENT PUBLIC ACCOUNTANTS

THE 1994 ABBOTT LABORATORIES PROXY STATEMENT WILL BE FILED WITH THE COMMISSION UNDER SEPARATE COVER ON OR ABOUT 3/4/94

OTHER CORPORATE EVENTS

ELECTION OF THIRTEEN DIRECTORS, ANNUAL SHAREHOLDERS MEETING, 04/29/94 (10Q 03/31/94)

•

•

•

RATIFICATION OF ARTHUR ANDERSEN & CO AS AUDITOR, ANNUAL SHAREHOLDERS MEETING, 04/29/94 (10Q 03/31/94)

REJECTION, PROPOSAL REGARDING INFANT FORMULA SUPPLY TO HOSPITALS (10Q 03/31/94

APPROVAL, AMENDING BYLAWS, BY BOARD OF DIRECTORS, 04/16/93 (10Q 06/30/83)

FIGURE 7-1 (continued)

PRESIDENT'S LETTER

(FROM ANNUAL REPORT TO SHAREHOLDERS)

REPORT TO SHAREHOLDERS

1993 Performance

In a year characterized by exceptional turbulence and uncertainty in many of the markets we serve, Abbott's operating results in 1993 were excellent. Net sales increased 7.1 percent while earnings per share increased 15 percent over 1992, one of the strongest performances in our industry.

•

•

•

Our purpose remains constant today. In fact, it has never been more appropriate. As in the past, our future will depend on our ability to innovate. We are confident that our people, supported by a high level of investment, will chart the only course that will accommodate worldwide needs to improve health care while controlling the rate of growth of health care costs: That course is innovation.

Duane L. Burnham, Chairman and Chief Executive Officer

Thomas R. Hodgson, President and Chief Operating Officer
February 24, 1994

MANAGEMENT DISCUSSION

(EXHIBIT 13)

ABBOTT LABORATORIES AND SUBSIDIARIES

FINANCIAL REVIEW

December 31, 1993

RESULTS OF OPERATIONS: Worldwide sales increased 7.1 percent in 1993 due to unit growth of 8.6 percent and net price increases of .9 percent, partially offset 2.4 percent by the effect of the relatively stronger U.S. dollar. Sales increased 14.2 percent in 1992 due to unit growth of 10.6 percent and net price increases of 2.9 percent. In 1991, sales increased 11.7 percent due to unit growth of 8.9 percent and net price increases of 2.9 percent.

•

•

•

LEGISLATIVE ISSUES: The Company's primary markets are highly competitive and subject to substantial government regulation. In the U.S., comprehensive legislation may be enacted that would make significant changes to the availability, delivery and payment for health care products and services. International operations are also subject to a significant degree of government regulation. It is not possible to predict the extent to which the Company or the health care industry in general might be adversely affected by these factors in the future. A more complete discussion of these factors is contained in Item 1, Business, in the Annual Report on Form 10K, which is available upon request.

FIGURE 7-1 (continued)

FOOTNOTES

(SOURCE 10K)
NOTES TO CONSOLIDATED FINANCIAL STATEMENTS
ABBOTT LABORATORIES AND SUBSIDIARIES
Note 1—Summary of Significant Accounting Policies
Basis of Consolidation:
The consolidated financial statements include the accounts of the parent company and subsidiaries, after elimination of intercompany transactions. The accounts of foreign subsidiaries are consolidated as of November 30.

Cash and Cash Equivalents:
Cash equivalents consist of time deposits and certificates of deposit with original maturities of three months or less. The carrying amount of cash and cash equivalents approximated fair value as of December 31, 1993 and 1992.

•

•

•

Earnings per Common Share:
Earnings per common share amounts are computed using the weighted average number of common shares outstanding.

Note 2—Debt and Lines of Credit

The following is a summary of longterm debt at December 31:
(dollalrs in thousands)

	1993	1992	1991
5.6% debentures, due 2003	$200,000	$ – – – –	$ – – – –
Industrial revenue bonds at various rates of interest, averaging 4.0% at December 31, 1993, and due at various dates through 2023	82,600	82,600	82,600
Other, principally foreign affiliate borrowings at various rates of interest, averaging 4.7% at December 31, 1993, and due at various dates through 1998	22,240	27,418	45,518
Total, net of current maturities	306,840	110,018	125,118
Current maturities of longterm debt	2,080	7,147	20,724
Total carrying amount	$308,920	$117,165	$145,842
Total fair market value	$304,038	$115,568	

•

•

•

Instructions on the Use of the Disclosure Database[1]

To begin the use of the *Disclosure Database* in your research, with the DOS A prompt (A>) on the screen, insert your Disclosure diskette in drive A and type **Disc**. The Introduction to Disclosure should then appear on your screen.

Next, notice the *Select Search Mode* display. The three items appearing are:

1. *Easy Menu Mode*—This menu provides the search capabilities of the Disclosure Database. The Easy Menu Mode will guide you through the initial search, modifications to the search, and the displaying and printing of the search results. At any point during a menu search, you may press the [F1] key for additional information, such as field content and how the field should be searched.
2. *Transfer Utilities*—This menu provides the options to convert downloaded data for further use with a spreadsheet file, a database file, or a mailing label file. However, for this student version this function will generally not be utilized.
3. *Return to DOS*—This option allows you to exit the Disclosure Database and return to the DOS prompt.

Accessing the Easy Menu Mode. Accessing the Easy Menu Mode displays the Main Activity Menu. Note that from this screen you can begin a search, obtain a description of the database, or quit the Easy Menu Mode.

Main Activity Menu

```
┌─────────────────────────────────────────────────┐
│          Select Main Activity                   │
├─────────────────────────────────────────────────┤
│ ►Begin a New Search (clears existing search)    │
│  Database Description Help                       │
│  Quit Easy Menu Mode                            │
└─────────────────────────────────────────────────┘
         Press F1 for Help Information
  F1-Help  ↑-↓ -Move        ←┘-Select       F9-Restart
```

Select *Begin A New Search* to access the Main Search Menu.

---

1   These instructions are from Disclosure's *Compact Disclosure User's Manual*. Reprinted with permission from Disclosure Incorporated.

Main Search Menu

```
┌─────────────────────────────────────────────────────┐
│              You can search by:                      │
├─────────────────────────────────────────────────────┤
│                                                       │
│   Company Name, Ticker or Number                      │
│   Type of Business                                    │
│   Geographic Area                                     │
│   Financial Information                               │
│   Full Text Fields                                    │
│   Number of Shares/Employees                          │
│   Owners, Officers, Directors                         │
│   Stock Exchange                                      │
│   Fortune Number                                      │
│   Use Previously Saved Search                         │
│   More Search Choices                                 │
│                                                       │
└─────────────────────────────────────────────────────┘
          Beginning a New Search
F1-Help  ↑-↓-Move  ↵-Select  F9-Restart  Esc-Prev Menu
```

All searching in the Easy Menu Mode option is conducted through a series of submenus and search windows. Three different types of windows exist: numeric, text, and index or dictionary.

1. *Numeric Searching*—Searching for any of the financial line items in the annual and quarterly balance sheet and income statement of cash flows, annual ratios, and stock price information is considered numeric searching. After a financial item has been selected for searching, the [F1] key can be pressed for additional help. See Figure 7-2 for general rules on numeric searching.

2. *Text Searching*—The applicable fields once selected may be searched for individual words, multiple words, or phrases. Additionally, word relationships can be specified. Applicable fields include:

All Text Fields	Auditor's Report
Corporate Exhibits Text	Cross Reference Name
Description of Business	Financial Comments Text
Financial Footnotes Text	Management Discussion Text
Name, Subsidiary, or X-ref	Other Corporate Events Text
President's Letter Text	Subsidiary Name
Words in Company Name	

FIGURE 7-2   General Rules for Numeric Searching

1. All financials are displayed in thousands, with the exception of outstanding shares and stock price data, which are in unit numbers. All numbers are searched in real terms.

2. All financial items are specified for search purposes with the two left-most significant digits.

   For example, to locate companies with $355,123,000 in net sales, enter 350000000.

3. It is not necessary to use commas when entering financial values.

4. When entering line item numbers, you may use T for trillion, B for billion, M for million, and K for thousand.

   For example, to locate companies with $355,123,000 in net sales, enter 350M.

5. Fields that contain decimal numbers are ratios, sources and uses of funds, and the weekly price earnings information sections of the company record. Decimal fields are searchable by the two left-most significant digits, regardless of their relationship to the decimal point.

   For example, to locate the value .0234, enter .023 because 2 and 3 are the left-most significant digits.

6. When searching for negative values

   a. Enter the number with the minus (-) sign. For example, negative one million would be entered as -1M.

   b. To search a range of negative numbers, enter the largest absolute value as the low value and the smallest absolute value as the maximum value.

   c. For a negative-to-positive range search, enter the negative value as the low end of the range and the positive value as the high end.

To search for a single word, simply enter the word and press Return. To search for synonyms, separate multiple entries with a comma. The search will include word one OR word two. For example, if you enter the words *newspaper, magazine* the search will retrieve newspaper or magazine.

Terms in relationship to each other may also be searched. A period (.) can be inserted between terms to indicate distance between word one and word two. For example, *executive...plan* will locate records where there are up to three words between *executive* and *plan*. An underline (_) may be inserted between terms to indicate the terms must be in the same sentence. An asterisk (*) may be inserted between terms to indicate that the terms must be located in the same field.

3. *Index/Dictionary Searching*—Each time one of the applicable fields is selected, a window appears on the screen. Applicable fields include:

All Text Fields	Auditor's Report
Auditor Change	City
Business Segment Text	Dictionary-List
Company Officer Name	DUNS Number
Director/Nominee Name	Fiscal Year End
Exchange	Fortune Number-List
Full Company Name	Legal Counsel
Location of Incorporation	Owner Name
Primary/Other SIC Code-List	Record Date-List
Rotated Company Name	State
Stock Transfer Agent	Telephone Area Code
Ticker Symbol	Zip Code
Auditor's Name	

As the search term is entered, the index of terms for the field is displayed in the window. To scroll through the index, use the Up/Dn Arrow keys or the Pg Up/Pg Dn keys. When you have located the desired term, press Return. The records containing the term will be retrieved and the term will be "marked" with an asterisk. The number of items selected and the total number of companies retrieved are displayed in the bottom right-hand corner of the screen.

To return the cursor to the beginning of the prompt, press the [F3] key. After all records have been selected, press the [F10] key for the Display/Print Menu.

Saving a Search.   To save a search strategy, key in your search steps and then select the *Save Search Strategy for Later Use* menu option. You'll be prompted for a file name; enter a unique name of eight or fewer characters. Precede the name with a drive designation to save your search on a drive other than the default drive.

To run a saved search, select *Previously Saved Search* from the main *You Can Search By:* menu. Next, highlight the saved search you wish to use from the menu list that will be displayed and press Return.

Displaying/Printing Search Results.   After your search has been conducted, the system presents an option to display or print any or all information.

The *Display/Print* option presents a menu of 17 predefined and 2 user-defined report/format choices. Use the [F8] key to access print or transfer (disk-capture) options while displaying the data on the screen.

Summary

Computerized databases provide an efficient and effective way of conducting accounting and auditing research. Your search is generally comprehensive and your time commitment is minimized. The *Disclosure SEC Database* presented in this chapter is one of many databases available to the accounting or auditing researcher.

Discussion Questions

The following questions are to be answered using your *Disclosure SEC Database* disk.

1. Which of the companies are listed on the New York Stock Exchange?

2. Did any company pay its officers more than $1 million individually in compensation?

3. Which of the companies have gross profit

5. Which companies use the LIFO inventory method?

6. Did any company report lawsuits or contingencies in its financial statements? (Hint: This is normally disclosed in the footnotes.)

7. Which companies reported treasury stock in their financial statements?

8. Did any company receive a qualified audit report?

9. Which companies were audited by Ernst & Young?

10. Which companies reported fully diluted earnings per share? What were the items resulting in diluted earnings?

REFINING THE RESEARCH PROCESS

Learning Objectives

After completing this chapter, you should understand:

- How to execute the five basic steps in the research process introduced in Chapter 1.

- The three stages in identifying the issue or problem to research.

- How to review related accounting or auditing literature—collect the evidence.

- The preparation of keyword/citation diagrams and reference matrix.

- The importance of professional judgment in evaluating the results of your research.

- How a research memorandum documents the results of your research process.

- How to prepare a research summary worksheet.

- How to "keep current" with the ever-expanding body of accounting and auditing pronouncements.

The preceding chapters have laid the foundation for conducting efficient and effective applied accounting and auditing research. At this point in the text, the reader should be familiar with the various manual and computerized research tools and should have a clear understanding of the basic five-step research process introduced in Chapter 1.

This chapter expands upon the application of these steps by applying them to a comprehensive problem that illustrates the research process in detail. Specific steps and procedures for conducting and documenting the research process are summarized in Figure 8-1, which presents a flow chart depicting an overview of the complete research process. Each step should be executed and documented for every research project.

Method of Conducting Research

The foundation for practical accounting and auditing research has now been set. The practitioner will generally be confronted with problems relating to proper accounting treatment for given transactions or the proper financial presentation of accounting data and disclosures. The focus of the research will be to determine the appropriate alternative principles, locate authoritative support for those alternatives, and apply professional judgment in selecting one principle from the list of alternatives. What the researcher now needs is a systematic method for conducting research.

The following is an illustrative problem that is used to demonstrate the application of the research methodology depicted in Figure 8-1. The problem and research steps should be followed carefully in order to comprehend the complete research process.

> Keller Realty, Inc., is a national real estate firm. The firm was incorporated in 19X6, and Alex Keller, the founder and president, is the majority stockholder. In 19X8, Keller decided to expand his successful regional real estate firm into a national operation. He established offices in major cities across the country. The corporation leased all of the office space. The standard lease agreement included a ten-year, noncancellable term and a five-year option renewable at the discretion of the lessee.
>
> During the years 19Y0-Y2, the residential home market became severely depressed due to tight monetary policies and high interest rates. Because of the depressed market, Keller decided to eliminate 25 offices located in depressed economic areas that he believed would not experience a recovery in the housing market in the succeeding five years. In 19Y2, Keller Realty, Inc., did close the 25 offices. The realty company,

FIGURE 8-1   Overview of the Research Process

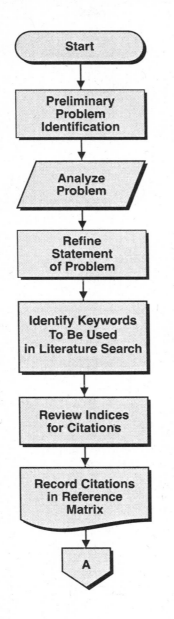

Problem can result from a new transaction, new pronouncement, change in the economic environment of the company, etc. Research can be conducted before or after the critical event has occurred.

Review relevant documentation and interview personnel involved. Identify the nature of the event and the economic impact on the parties involved.

Succinctly state the problem in a way that will facilitate analysis and generate several keywords.

Keywords should flow from the problem statement. Use a broad sample of keywords to address all aspects of the problem.

The *Index to Accounting and Auditing Technical Pronouncements*, the topical index to the *Professional Standards*, and the topical index to the FASB's *Current Text* are examples of appropriate indices. Alternatively, a NAARS computer search could be used to locate citations.

FIGURE 8-1 (continued)

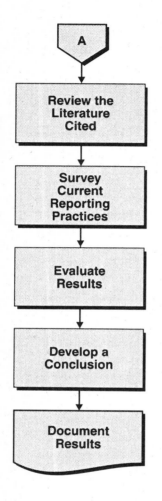

The official pronouncements of the CAP, APB, and FASB should be reviewed first. AICPA Interpretations and Comments in the TIS and FASB Technical Bulletins can also be reviewed to clarify the promulgated standards.

Review *Financial Report Surveys, Accounting Trends & Techniques,* or the NAARS database for current reporting and disclosure practices.

Evaluate the literature in terms of the applicability to the research problem and the weight of authoritative support. Identify alternatives and, if appropriate, consult with associates or the client.

The conclusion should be a determination of the proper accounting and reporting procedures based upon research findings.

Documentation consists of the statement of the problem; summary of the transaction or event and its economic impact on the company; reference matrix; summary of relevant literature; basis of conclusion; journal entries; financial statement presentations; and disclosures.

however, was bound by the lease agreements on all these offices.
The company was able to sublease 10 of the offices but continued to make lease payments on the 15 remaining vacated ones.

The lease commitments have been properly classified as
operating leases. The controller for the company, Elaine Wise,
has expressed concern to Keller about the proper accounting
for the lease commitments on the 15 offices that have not
been subleased. Wise feels that the future lease commitments
should be recognized as a loss for the current period. However, Keller disagrees and believes that the rental payments
are period costs that should be recognized as expense in the
year paid. Keller is confident that the vacant offices can be
subleased within the next year, and there is no need to book a
loss and corresponding liability in this accounting period. He
has, however, given the controller the task of researching this
problem and making a recommendation supported by current
authoritative pronouncements. Elaine has asked your firm,
Arthur & Young, CPAs, to help in the development of the
recommendation.

Step 1—Identify the Issue or Problem. Identification of the issue or
problem, a critical step in the research process, is too often given the least attention. A clear and concise statement of the issue is important to begin the research
process. This step can be subdivided into three stages:

1. Preliminary problem identification
2. Problem analysis
3. Refined statement of the problem

Preliminary Problem Identification. This simply means that a potential
problem must be recognized before any action will be taken to solve it. The
initial step in the research process, therefore, is identification of a potential problem. In this example, the controller has recognized a potential problem in the
accounting and reporting treatment of lease commitments on vacated offices. It
should be noted that the president, Alex Keller, does not agree that a problem
exists. He believes the fact that the offices are vacant does not change the nature
of the lease commitment, and that there is no need for changing the established
accounting and reporting procedures. It is the problem recognition by the controller that initiates the entire research process.

The initial statement of the problem could be written as follows: "Should a
loss be recognized in the current period from lease commitments on vacant
offices?"

Problem Analysis. The controller examines the lease agreements and finds the following information:

1. The lease agreements were prepared by Karen Roth, attorney for Keller Realty, Inc. All the leases were standardized, and the details were filled in for specific locations.
2. The terms of the lease require the lessee to make all the monthly payments over the noncancellable term or find a sublessee suitable to the lessor.
3. A summary of the lease commitments was prepared by the controller as follows:

Number of Leases	Monthly Rental Rate	Remaining Noncancellable Terms in Months	Total Commitment
10	$1,500	60	$900,000
5	$2,500	60	$750,000

4. In discussing the lease agreements with the lawyer, the controller learned that Keller Realty, Inc., is bound by the terms of the leases and would probably be sued by the lessors and forced to make the lease payments if the company dishonored its commitment.
5. Ken Riley, the general manager at the company headquarters, is responsible for subleasing the vacated offices. In a discussion with the controller, he indicated that it is highly unlikely that all of the vacant offices would be subleased. He explained that the 10 offices that had been subleased are in areas that have not been severely depressed. The remaining 15 offices will be more difficult to sublease. He feels confident that he can sublease five offices by the middle of the next fiscal year, but doubts that the remaining properties can be subleased. Under the terms of existing subleases, the monthly rent paid by the sublessees equals the rent expense that the realty company was obligated to pay under the original leases. Riley indicated that each of the five additional offices that he expects to sublease can be rented for the $1,500 per month currently paid by the realty company.
6. The company's incremental borrowing rate is currently 12%.

After considering the information gathered through a review of the lease documents and discussions with the lawyer and the office manager, the controller concludes that the economic impact is contingent upon the ability of the company to sublease the vacant offices. It is clear that the costs incurred to make lease payments on the vacant offices represent a loss to the company, since no revenues are being generated from these units. The controller feels that she can rely upon the office manager's ability to estimate the number of offices that will not be subleased.

Refined Statement of Problem. After the analysis, the controller restates the research problem as follows:

> "Should a contingent loss be recognized currently on future rental commitments on vacant offices, and, if so, what amounts should be recognized?"

Step 2—Collect Evidence. The collection of evidence generally involves (1) a review of related accounting or auditing literature and (2) a survey of present practice.

Review of Accounting or Auditing Literature. The review of the literature should begin with the pronouncements of official standard-setting bodies— generally the FASB and AICPA or, in certain cases, the SEC, CASB, or the GASB. It is important to note the scope of any pronouncements reviewed. Time should not be spent in a detailed review of pronouncements that are not applicable to the transaction under investigation. However, pronouncements that do not specifically address the research problem, but are related to it, should not be completely ignored. They can be reviewed for possible references to other appropriate sources; discussions within these pronouncements may add insights into the problem at hand. If these primary sources do not provide the needed accounting or auditing information, then the search must extend to secondary authoritative sources such as industrial practices, published research studies, and other sources. The researcher should begin the review of primary sources and those that have the highest level of authority as indicated by the hierarchy of GAAP. Once the researcher has exhausted the primary sources, then he/she proceeds to review any secondary sources.

A list of keywords is essential to locating relevant authoritative literature. The reader should note that a good problem statement will generate the initial keywords necessary to begin to access the appropriate sections of the professional literature. After the search has begun, additional keywords may be identified. From the analysis and statement of the problem, the controller identifies the following keywords to be used in the literature search:

Losses	Contingent Loss
Loss Recognition	Leases
Commitments	Rent Expense

Using keywords to locate citations is akin to traveling through a maze, with the researcher encountering cross references that circle back to original starting points and keywords that prove to be dead ends. The literature search must be conducted carefully and systematically; otherwise, the process can be frustrating and inefficient. The *Index to Accounting and Auditing Technical Pronouncements* will be used to demonstrate a systematic approach to conducting the literature search.

Figure 8-2 diagrams one path that could be taken through the *Index*. The diagram aids the researcher in conducting and documenting an efficient literature search. The starting point of the search is the list of keywords identified from the statement of the problem. As these terms are reviewed for relevant citations, cross-references to other terms—broader, narrower, or related—are found in the *Index*. These additional terms are then examined for potential citations. The *Index* citations are listed alphabetically by authoritative source. The reader can determine the authoritative weight of each citation directly from the hierarchy of GAAP presented in Chapter 3. The researcher would want to start with the highest level of primary authoritative literature. If an answer is found in a primary authoritative pronouncement, the researcher can stop the research process. Otherwise, the researcher must continue the review of secondary sources.

When the researcher feels that all relevant citations have been identified, the next step is to locate and review the authoritative literature. All the citations in Figure 8-2 reference sections of the *FASB Accounting Standards—Current Text.*[1]

Section C59, "Contingencies," includes two relevant authoritative pronouncements—FASB Statement No. 5 and FASB Interpretation No. 14. The Topical Index of the *Current Text* can be used to locate specific paragraphs within this section. The paragraph references are located in the Topical Index under the keyword "Contingencies." It should be noted that the keywords used in topical indexes do not necessarily correspond to those used in the *Index to Accounting and Auditing Technical Pronouncements*. A reference matrix similar to that shown in Figure 8-3 can be constructed to facilitate identification of section references and original pronouncements.

Following is a summary of the relevant portions of the literature:

> A loss contingency as defined in FASB Statement No. 5, paragraph 1, is "an existing condition, situation, or set of circumstances involving uncertainty as to possible . . . loss . . . to an enterprise that will ultimately be resolved when one or more future events occur or fail to occur."

FASB Statement No. 5, paragraph 8, states that "[an] estimated loss from a loss contingency . . . should be accrued by a charge to income if both of the following conditions are met:

> a. . . . it is probable that . . . [a loss has] been incurred . . . [i.e., it is probable that] future events will occur confirming the fact of the loss.

---

1   The reference coding of the citations in the *Index to Accounting and Auditing Technical Pronouncements* correlates with the coding in the *FASB Accounting Standards—Current Text* as follows (also see Appendix A at the end of this chapter):

	INDEX	**CURRENT TEXT**
FASB Statements	FAS	FAS
FASB Interpretations	FASI	FIN
FASB Technical Bulletins	FAST	FTB

FIGURE 8-2 Keyword/Citation Diagram

Keyword	Cross-References	Reference Descriptions	Citation
Losses	NT Abandoned Lease Costs	No Relevant Citations	
U Costs	RT Cost Allocation	No Relevant Citations	
	NT Loss Adjustment Expense	No Relevant Citations	
Loss Recognition		Original Lessees	FASI 27.02/L10
		Subleases not involving...	FAST 79-15/L10
Commitments	RT Contingencies	No Relevant Citations	
	RT Contingent Liabilities	No Relevant Citations	
		Contingencies...	AUIJ01-76/9509[2]
		FAS 5 Effect	
		Contingencies and... Range of Loss	FASI 14.02/C59
Contingency Loss (Not Used)			
Leases	NT Noncancellable Leases	Accounting & Reporting	FASI 13.00/L10
	NT Subleases	No Relevant Citations	
		Original Lessees	FASI 27.02/L10
		Loss Recognition	FAST 79-15/L10
Rent Expense		No Relevant Citations	

2   The reference coding AUIJ in the *Index to Accounting and Auditing Technical Pronouncements* is the abbreviation for AICPA Auditing Interpretations. The 01-76 refers to the issue date (month and year) of the interpretation. The 9509 is the coding for the auditing interpretation section in the *AICPA Professional Standards*.

FIGURE 8-3   Reference Matrix

Keyword	Current Text Section	Reference FASB Statement No. 5	FASB Interpretation No. 14
Contingencies Loss Contingencies	C59.105–.107 C59.109–.110 C59.124–.127	Par. 8 Par. 9–10	Par. 2–3 Par.4–7
Description of Term	C59.101	Par. 1	
Range of Loss	C59.109 C59.124—.127	Par. 10	Par. 4–7
Loss Contingency Classification	C59.104	Par. 3	

  b. The amount of loss can be reasonably estimated."

  FASB Interpretation No. 14 clarifies the point that a loss should be accrued even if no single amount for the loss can be estimated. If only a range of potential loss can be estimated, the minimum amount should be accrued.

  After reviewing relevant sections in the *Current Text*, the researcher could read the original pronouncements—FASB Statement No. 5 and Interpretation No. 14 —to obtain additional insight into the background and rationale underlying the standards.

  Survey of Present Practice.   In addition to the review of authoritative literature, Step 2 involves determining how other companies with similar circumstances or transactions have handled the accounting and reporting procedures. This survey could include a review of *Accounting Trends & Techniques* or *Financial Reporting Surveys* as well as a discussion of the issue with colleagues via the Internet.

Step 3—Evaluate Results and Identify Alternatives.   This step requires the exercise of professional judgment. The evidence should be carefully reviewed and one or more tentative conclusions identified. The quality and amount of authoritative support for each alternative should be evaluated. In addition, the evidence may be reviewed with other accountants knowledgeable in the field.

The initial concern was whether to recognize any loss currently on the lease commitments on vacant offices. Through the examination of related documents and discussions with persons involved with the transactions, the following facts were identified:

1. The realty company has an enforceable obligation to make the lease payments on the vacant offices.
2. The payments will represent a loss to the company because no revenues will be generated by the costs incurred.
3. The amount of the loss is contingent upon the ability of the realty company to sublease the offices. A reasonable estimate is that a maximum of five buildings could be subleased, and it is possible that none will be subleased.

The literature search has provided authoritative support for recognizing a contingent loss. The amount of the loss is to be measured by the minimum amount for the range of the estimated loss. There was no support in the literature for considering the rental payments as period costs to be recognized as expense when paid. In Figure 8-2, the *Current Text* section L10 was identified as a reference. FASB Technical Bulletin 79-15, which is an unofficial interpretation of FASB Statement No. 13, is cross-referenced to paragraphs .518–.520 of Section L10.[3] The interpretation addresses the loss on a sublease not involved in a disposal of a business segment. It states that a loss should be recognized in a sublease in order to follow the general principle of providing for losses when it is reasonable to assume they have occurred. This same reasoning can be extended to the problem at hand where there will be no sublease payments to reduce the amount of the loss.

Step 4—Develop Conclusion.
If the evaluation process is properly performed, the researcher should be able to develop a well-reasoned, well-supported conclusion as to the appropriate resolution of the issue. In the illustrative problem, the authoritative literature found through the research process supports accrual of the loss on the lease agreements. The amount of the loss should be the minimum of the range of the contingent loss. The financial statements should disclose the nature of the contingent loss and the amount of potential loss above the amount accrued in the financial statements.

Step 5—Communicate Results.
Once the researcher has determined a solution to the research problem, the conclusion should be presented concisely and clearly to the client. Generally, a research memorandum serves as this communication medium, as follows:

---

3 See Appendix A in the FASB Accounting Standards—*Current Text* for the cross-referencing.

To: Alex Keller, President

From: Elaine Wise, Controller and Arthur & Young, CPAs

At your request, we have researched the following matter to determine the impact on Keller Realty. The specific issue researched concerns whether a loss should be recognized currently on the rental commitments on the vacant offices. If recognition is required, what amount should be accrued?

In researching the authoritative literature, the following keywords were utilized: Losses, Loss Recognition, Commitments, Contingent Loss, Leases, and Rent Expense. FASB Statement No. 5, "Accounting for Contingencies," states that a loss contingency should be accrued by a charge to income if (1) it is probable that a loss has been incurred and (2) the amount of the loss can be reasonably estimated. FASB Interpretation No. 14, "Reasonable Estimate of the Amount of Loss," states that when no single amount for the loss can be estimated, the minimum amount of loss should be accrued.

Keller Realty, Inc., has an enforceable obligation to make the lease payments on the vacant offices, and no revenues will be generated by the costs incurred. It is reasonably estimated that from zero to five buildings could be subleased. The authoritative literature supports the accrual of a loss for the vacant lease offices. The amount of the loss will be the minimum estimate of the range of potential loss. Since the lease obligations extend over more than one accounting period, the accrual will be at the present value of the lease payments discounted at the Realty Company's marginal borrowing rate.

	Number of Leases	Monthly Rate	Months	P.V. Factor of Annuity Due at 1%	P.V. Amount*
Additional units:					
Subleased..	5	$1500	3**	2.9704	$ 22,278
Not subleased ..	5	1500	60	45.4046	340,534
Not subleased..	5	2500	60	45.4046	567,557
Loss accrual.......					$ 930,369
Potential additional loss...	5	$1500	57	43.720	327,900
					$1,258,269
Current portion	5	$1500	3	2.9704	$ 22,278
of loss	5	1500	12	11.3676	85,257
recognized..	5	2500	12	11.3676	142,095
					$249,630

* P.V. Amount = (Number of Leases x Monthly Rate x P.V. Factor).

**Since 5 units are expected to be subleased within 6 months, the vacancy period on these units is averaged at 3 months.

The financial statement presentation and proper footnote disclosure should appear as follows:

<u>Financial Statement Presentation and Disclosure</u>

```
Income statement:
Revenues ......................................     XXXXX
Operating expenses
   Loss on lease commitments .................     $930,369
Balance sheet:
Current liabilities:
   Current portion of lease commitments .......    $249,630
   Long-term portion of lease commitments.......     680,739
```

<u>Notes</u>

Contingent Liabilities--The company has entered into certain lease agreements that have 5-year noncancellable terms remaining. Some of these offices are currently neither used nor subleased. The present value of the potential rental liability above the amount accrued is $327,900.

Documentation of the Research Process

Thorough documentation is a crucial part of the entire research process. The documentation should include:

1. A statement of the problem and relevant facts.
2. References to authoritative literature used.
3. A description of alternative procedures considered and the authoritative support for each alternative.
4. An explanation of why certain alternatives were discarded and why the recommended principle or procedure was selected.

Figure 8-4 contains an example of a documentation worksheet that the accounting firm might use to organize the pertinent research information for its records.

Keeping Current

In concluding this text, the authors would like to emphasize the importance of keeping current with the ever-expanding accounting and auditing pronouncements and to share with the reader some techniques that have been used successfully by various practitioners. Adopting one or a combination of the following techniques may save valuable time—to spend possibly on the golf course—rather than reading volume upon volume of materials in an attempt to stay current.

FIGURE 8-4   Documentation Worksheet of Accounting/Auditing Research

Client Information Name: Keller Realty, Inc. Address: 1300 W 5th St. New York, NY Client Code # K143 I. Problem Identification Scope or Statement of Problem: Should a contingent loss be recognized currently on future rental commitments on vacant offices? Contact Person (Client): Elaine Wise—Controller	II. Research Evidence Keywords Utilized: Loses (No Cites noted) Contingent Loss Loss Recognition Leases Commitments Rent Expense References (Citations): FASB No. 5, Par 8–10 FASB Interp. No 14, Par 2–7 FASB Tech Bulletin No. 79–15. FASB No. 13 Database (Library Resources) Utilized: FASB Stds—Current Text Accounting Trends & Techniques NAARS	III. Alternatives Available No other alternatives are permissible IV. Brief Summary of Conclusions The authoritative literature requires the accrual of its loss on the lease agreements. The amount should be the minimum of the range of the contingent loss.

1. **Checklists**—Some practitioners develop a checklist for keeping current. A listing of new pronouncements is prepared and updated periodically with an indication as to which clients a pronouncement may affect. Pronouncements having no direct immediate impact on any client are placed in a "rainy day" reading file.
2. **Pronouncement summaries**—Some firms have developed in-house staff memos that are prepared by certain individuals periodically (e.g., weekly) and distributed to all staff members. Such memos identify new pronouncements and provide a brief summary write-up of each new pronouncement.
3. **Reading of periodicals**—Many business and accounting periodicals report summaries or the full text of new pronouncements. The practice of reading certain periodicals, such as the *Journal of Accountancy, Management Accounting,* and the *Wall Street Journal,* will aid the practitioner in the attempt to keep current.
4. **Accounting newsletters**—Many organizations publish accounting newsletters to update the practitioner on current events. Major newsletters available include the following:

   - *The CPA Letter.* This newsletter published by the AICPA contains current information concerning the profession. Such topics include AICPA board business, new pronouncements on accounting and auditing, disciplinary actions against members, upcoming events, and briefs on events in Washington.
   - *FASB Status Report.* This monthly publication issued by the Financial Accounting Standards Board covers FASB official action and releases. The agenda of the FASB is periodically reported in addition to summary comments on recently issued statements, exposure drafts, or technical bulletins.
   - *Action Alert.* A weekly publication of the FASB on actions and future meetings.
   - *GASB Action Report.* Similar in contents to the FASB newsletter, this publication of the Governmental Accounting Standards Board issues quarterly reports of the GASB comments on GASB statements, exposure drafts, interpretations, or technical bulletins.

5. **Internet**—Utilizing the newsgroups on the Internet can keep you abreast of topics of interest to you and your clients.

Keeping up to date on the details of all new pronouncements is an impossibility. However, every practitioner must develop and consistently use a technique to keep as current as possible, especially with pronouncements that directly affect clients.

Summary

The accountant or auditor who attempts to keep current and has developed skills in researching accounting and auditing issues will be well rewarded by having obtained the confidence and respect of management and colleagues. Such respect is generally reserved for the truly professional accountant or auditor. This text attempts to aid the practitioner in fulfilling his or her professional role, which includes that of a competent researcher in accounting and auditing matters.

Discussion Questions

1. What is the focus of accounting and auditing research?

2. What are the three components used to identify the problem or issue?

3. Explain two ways to collect evidence.

4. How are keywords used to evaluate and collect evidence?

5. What is the purpose of a research memorandum?

6. What are two common causes of accounting problems?

7. What should be included in the documentation of the research process?

8. What are some basic ways of keeping current with the authoritative literature?

APPENDIX A
Abbreviations Used in Citations

Abbreviation	Title of Pronouncement
AAG-APC	Audit and Accounting Guide, Audits of Agricultural Producers and Agricultural Cooperatives
AAG-BRD	Audit and Accounting Guide: Audits of Brokers and Dealers in Securities
AAG-CAS	Audit and Accounting Guide: Audits of Casinos
AAG-CON	Audit and Accounting Guide: Construction Contractors
AAG-CRU	Audit and Accounting Guide: Audits of Credit Unions
AAG-EBP	Audit and Accounting Guide: Audits of Employee Benefit Plans
AAG-FGC	Audit and Accounting Guide: Audits of Federal Government Contractors
AAG-FIN	Audit and Accounting Guide: Audits of Financial Companies (Including Independent and Captive Financing Activities of Other Companies)
AAG-HCS	Audit and Accounting Guide: Audits of Providers of Health Care Services
AAG-INV	Audit and Accounting Guide: Audits of Investment Companies
AAG-NPR	Audit and Accounting Guide: Audits of Certain Nonprofit Organizations
AAG-OGP	Audit and Accounting Guide: Audits of Entities with Oil and Gas Producing Activities
AAG-PLI	Audit and Accounting Guide: Audits of Property and Liability Insurance Companies
AAG-PRO	Audit and Accounting Guide: Guide for Prospective Financial Information
AAG-RLE	Audit and Accounting Guide: Guide for the Use of Real Estate Appraisal Information
AAG-SAM	Audit and Accounting Guide: Audit Sampling
AAG-SAV	Audit and Accounting Guide: Audits of Savings Institutions
AAG-SLG	Audit and Accounting Guide: Audits of State and Local Governmental Units
ACC-PB	Accounting Standards Division Practice Bulletins

ACC-SOP	Accounting Standards Division Statements of Position
ACIJ	AICPA Accounting Interpretations
APB	Accounting Principles Board Opinions
APBS	Accounting Principles Board Statements
ARB	Accounting Research Bulletins
ATB	Accounting Terminology Bulletins
AUD-SOP	Auditing Standards Division Statements of Position
AUG-AIR	Industry Audit Guide: Audits of Airlines
AUG-BNK	Industry Audit Guide: Audits of Banks
AUG-COL	Industry Audit Guide: Audits of Colleges and Universities
AUG-SLI	Industry Audit Guide: Audits of Stock Life Insurance Companies
AUG-VHW	Industry Audit Guide: Audits of Voluntary Health and Welfare Organizations
AUIJ	AICPA Auditing Interpretations
CASB	Cost Accounting Standards Board Standards
CASB-I	Cost Accounting Standards Board Interpretations
EPS	Computing Earnings Per Share
ET-INT	Ethics Interpretations of Rules of Conduct
ET-RLNG	Ethics Rulings
ET-RULE	Code of Professional Conduct—Rules
FAC	Financial Accounting Standards Board Statements of Financial Accounting Concepts
FAS	Financial Accounting Standards Board Statements of Financial Accounting Standards
FASEITF	Financial Accounting Standards Board Emerging Issues Task Force Consensus
FASI	Financial Accounting Standards Board Interpretations
FAST	Financial Accounting Standards Board Technical Bulletins
GAC	Governmental Accounting Standards Board Statement of Financial Accounting Concepts
GAS	Governmental Accounting Standards Board Statements on Governmental Accounting Standards
GASI	Governmental Accounting Standards Board Interpretations
GAST	Governmental Accounting Standards Board Technical Bulletins
GUD-PFS	Personal Financial Statements Guide

IAS	International Accounting Standards
IAU	International Statements on Auditing
IAU/RS	International Statements on Auditing/Related Services
NCGA	National Council on Governmental Accounting Statements
NCGAI	National Council on Governmental Accounting Interpretations
PFP	Statements on Responsibilities in Personal Financial Planning Practice
QC	Statements on Quality Control Standards
QCI	Quality Control Standards Interpretations
QR	Standards for Performing and Reporting on Quality Reviews
QRI	Quality Review Interpretations
SAR	Statements on Standards for Accounting and Review Services
SARI	Accounting and Review Services Interpretations
SAS	Statements on Auditing Standards
SEC-AAER	Accounting and Auditing Enforcement Releases
SEC-FRR	Financial Reporting Releases
SEC-SAB	Staff Accounting Bulletins
SECSK	Regulation S-K
SECSX	Regulation S-X
SSAE	Statement on Standards for Attestation Engagements
SSAEI	AICPA Attestation Engagements Interpretations
SSCS	Statements on Standards for Consulting Services